What on Earth Are We Here For?

God's Ultimate Plan for Man Revealed

by
Keith Butler

HARRISON HOUSE
Tulsa, Oklahoma

What on Earth Are We Here For?
God's Ultimate Plan for Man Revealed
ISBN 0-89274-947-4
Copyright © 1996 by Keith Butler
P. O. Box 760037
Lathrup Village, Michigan 48076-0037

Published by Harrison House, Inc.
P. O. Box 35035
Tulsa, Oklahoma 74153

Contents

Contents

Introduction

God has a plan for all of mankind, and He specifically has a plan for you as an individual. He established this plan in the beginning when He created the heaven and the earth and placed man in authority over this planet.

Today we are seeing so many problems and so much chaos throughout the world because people have gotten away from God's plan for their lives. In fact, much of the Church of the Lord Jesus Christ has stepped out of God's plan.

It's important that we realize God's plan for us and then determine to operate accordingly every day of our lives.

We will look into this subject of authority by starting our study in the book of Genesis. Genesis is often referred to as the book of beginnings. This is where we find God's plan for man.

When God created man, the first thing He did was to give man dominion and authority over all the earth. We will consider the authority that was given in the beginning and the authority that has been provided for the believer today by the Lord Jesus Christ. Every believer in Him must take the responsibility to live each day according to God's plan.

Now let's begin our study at the beginning as we discover God's plan for man.

1
God's Creation

In the beginning God created the heaven and the earth.

And the earth was without form, and void; and darkness was upon the face of the deep. And the Spirit of God moved upon the face of the waters.

Genesis 1:1,2

As verse 2 says, **The earth was without form, and void; and darkness was upon the face of the deep.** We know, however, that nothing God creates is dark and void; everything He creates is good. For the earth to be described as dark and void and without form shows us that something must have happened.

Before "The Beginning"

Like some theologians, I believe we have not been informed by God of everything there is to know about pre-earth or what happened in heaven.

Now this is just my opinion, and opinion is different from "Thus saith the Lord...." It's only speculation and I can't prove it, but I believe there was a passage of time between Genesis 1:1 and 1:2 when certain things occurred. I believe that this passage of time took place before Adam and Eve ever existed and that there was a civilization prior to them.

According to Scripture, there was a war in heaven. Satan (known then as an angelic being named Lucifer) was joined by a third of the angels to rebel against God. They, of course, lost the fight and were tossed out of heaven. That's when Satan and his host of angels were cast down to the earth. (See Rev. 12:3,4,7-9.) I believe when they came to this earth they destroyed everything that was here at that time.

Science and the Bible are not necessarily crosswise to one another. Dinosaurs and other creatures walked the earth before man. Then something bad happened. A terrible and cataclysmic event occurred on the earth and everything was wiped out. It was after that, I believe, when the earth was dark and void.

The Earth Was Replenished

Let's take a look at Genesis 1:28 for a moment. It says:

And God blessed them, and God said unto them, Be fruitful, and multiply, and replenish the earth....

Notice it says, **God blessed** *them,* **and God said unto** *them....* That means God was dealing with both the male and the female.

God was speaking to Adam and Eve, saying, "I want you to *replenish* the earth." To replenish means to restock. God was having man restock the earth.

We know what it's like at our house to replenish something. Frequently we have to replenish the refrigerator once our three teenagers have gotten into it, especially our eighteen-year-old son. When I was eighteen, I could eat all day long and never gain a pound. With three fairly good-sized kids at our house, we have to restock the refrigerator every few days because the supply is gone.

Adam and Eve being told to *replenish* the earth implies that there must have been something on the earth prior to them. Clearly, things had been deleted from the earth and there needed to be a restocking.

This has given us clues that much more had occurred in the beginning. The Word tells us, **We see through a glass,**

darkly (1 Cor. 13:12), so we are now seeing only a part of all the things concerning God and His creation.

The First Five Days of Creation

Day One

In Scripture, we can watch as each day unfolds:

> **In the beginning God created the heaven and the earth.**
>
> **And the earth was without form, and void; and darkness was upon the face of the deep. And the Spirit of God moved upon the face of the waters.**
>
> **And God said, Let there be light: and there was light.**
>
> Genesis 1:1-3

And God *said....* This is how God created everything: by speaking it into existence.

> **And God saw the light, that it was good: and God divided the light from the darkness.**
>
> **And God called the light Day, and the darkness he called Night. And the evening and the morning were the first day.**
>
> Genesis 1:4,5

Day Two

As we continue on in Scripture, day two unfolds with God's re-creation of the heavens in verses 6 through 8:

> **And God said, Let there be a firmament in the midst of the waters, and let it divide the waters from the waters.**
>
> **And God made the firmament, and divided the waters which were under the firmament from the waters which were above the firmament: and it was so.**
>
> **And God called the firmament Heaven. And the evening and the morning were the second day.**

Day Three

At that time this whole planet was nothing but water, so God divided the earth from the seas:

> **And God said, Let the waters under the heaven be gathered together unto one place, and let the dry land appear: and it was so.**
>
> **And God called the dry land Earth; and the gathering together of the waters called he Seas: and God saw that it was good.**
>
> **Genesis 1:9,10**

Then God said:

> **Let the earth bring forth grass, the herb yielding seed, and the fruit tree yielding fruit after his kind, whose seed is in itself, upon the earth: and it was so.**
>
> **And the earth brought forth grass, and herb yielding seed after his kind, and the tree yielding fruit, whose seed was in itself, after his kind....**
>
> **Genesis 1:11,12**

God intended for everything in the earth to reproduce after its own kind, because everything in the earth had been given the seed within itself to reproduce. This was God's plan for the whole planet before it was His plan for man. (We will consider the subject of seed in more detail later in this study.)

Now let's continue with the latter part of verse 12:

> **...and God saw that it was good.**
>
> **And the evening and the morning were the third day.**
>
> **Genesis 1:12,13**

Day Four

In day four God divided day from night:

> **And God said, Let there be lights in the firmament of the heaven to divide the day from the night; and let**

them be for signs, and for seasons, and for days, and years:

And let them be for lights in the firmament of the heaven to give light upon the earth: and it was so.

And God made two great lights; the greater light to rule the day, and the lesser light to rule the night: he made the stars also.

And God set them in the firmament of the heaven to give light upon the earth,

And to rule over the day and over the night, and to divide the light from the darkness: and God saw that it was good.

And the evening and the morning were the fourth day.

Genesis 1:14-19

On day four God put lights in the heavens, which we call stars. He set up the brightest light, the sun, to give light for the day and a lesser light, the moon, to give light for the night.

Day Five

And God said, Let the waters bring forth abundantly the moving creature that hath life, and fowl that may fly above the earth in the open firmament of heaven.

And God created great whales, and every living creature that moveth, which the waters brought forth abundantly, after their kind, and every winged fowl after his kind: and God saw that it was good.

And God blessed them, saying, Be fruitful, and multiply, and fill the waters in the seas, and let fowl multiply in the earth.

And the evening and the morning were the fifth day.

Genesis 1:20-23

God's will was for every species in this planet to be fruitful and multiply itself. That was day five.

"Seedtime and Harvest"

God spoke about this principle again when He was making a covenant with Noah. He said:

> **While the earth remaineth, seedtime and harvest, and cold and heat, and summer and winter, and day and night shall not cease.**
>
> **Genesis 8:22**

Notice particularly in this verse that there was seedtime and harvest.

You will never see a male and a female cat come together and produce a litter of dogs or mice. Cats produce only cats. Apple trees produce only apples. Orange trees produce only oranges. The seeds are in everything. Slice open an apple or an orange and you will find seeds to reproduce that particular fruit. That's God's plan for everything — including man.

Day Six: The Creation of Man

In verse 26 we go into the sixth day of God's creation — or re-creation — of the earth:

> **And God said, Let us make man in our image....**

When God said, **Let *us* make man**, who was He talking to?

To the angels? No. The angels weren't involved in making mankind.

To the devil? Certainly not! God wasn't in league with the devil.

Created in the Image and Likeness of God

The word *us* in this verse refers to the triunity of God — the Father, the Son and the Holy Ghost. The triune God was saying:

> **Let *us* make man in *our* image, after *our* likeness....**

The Hebrew word for *image* here, *tselem*, meaning "resemblance,"[1] is accompanied by *demûwth*, meaning "likeness."[2] "Likeness added to image tells us that the divine image that man bears is one corresponding to the original pattern."[3]

Created to Have Dominion Over the Earth

Let us make man in our image, after our likeness: *and let them have dominion* over the fish of the sea, and over the fowl of the air, and over the cattle, and over all the earth, and over every creeping thing that creepeth upon the earth.

Genesis 1:26

The first thing God did was to give man dominion over all the earth and everything in it. The word translated "dominion" is the Hebrew word, *radah*, which means to "rule" or to "reign."[4] God's original will and intention was for man, who was made in His image and likeness, to rule and reign over everything in this planet. God gave man authority over it all.

God's First Commandment to Man

So God created man in his own image, in the image of God created he him; male and female created he them.

And God blessed them, and God said unto them, *Be fruitful, and multiply, and replenish the earth*....

Genesis 1:27,28

Note that God's first commandment was for man to *be fruitful, and multiply, and replenish the earth*. God intended for mankind to perpetuate himself.

For this reason I must make a statement here that is clearly in opposition to the beliefs of a certain segment of today's society: Homosexuality is against God's will!

Homosexuality cannot be the will of God. It does not follow the principle God set out for man from the beginning.

Two men engaging in sex with one another will never produce anything. The same is true of the sexual relationship between two women. No children can ever be created by such a union. Nothing can come of it. God's plan is for everything on this planet to have the seed in itself to produce.

Now that's not to say God hates people who happen to be gay or lesbian. No, God doesn't hate them; He loves them. Neither are we to hate them; we too are to love them. But their lifestyle has never been a part of God's plan; and what isn't God's plan isn't right. The Creator's plan for mankind is the same as His original plan for this planet: that everything produce after its kind. (Gen. 1:11,24.)

Starting in the Old Testament and going all the way through the New Testament, God intended for His people as a whole to procreate and raise up a godly seed. That's why believers in Jesus Christ have been instructed to raise up their children in the nurture and admonition of the Lord. (Eph. 6:4.)

And God blessed them, and God said unto them, Be fruitful, and multiply, and replenish the earth, and subdue it: and have dominion over the fish of the sea, and over the fowl of the air, and over every living thing that moveth upon the earth.

Genesis 1:28

God Gave Man Seed for Harvest

I want you to notice God's original design before sin came into the earth through man's disobedience:

And God said, Behold, I have given you every herb bearing seed, which is upon the face of all the earth, and every tree, in the which is the fruit of a tree yielding seed; to you it shall be for meat.

And to every beast of the earth, and to every fowl of the air, and to every thing that creepeth upon the earth, wherein there is life, I have given every green herb for meat: and it was so.

And God saw every thing that he had made, and, behold, it was very good. And the evening and the morning were the sixth day.

Genesis 1:29-31

On day six when man was originally created by God, he was not carnivorous. Neither was any other creature at that time. God said, **To every beast of the earth** (meaning every lion, every tiger, every creature on the earth)...**I have given every green herb for meat.**

The way God designed things in the beginning is not the way things are today. It was only after sin and the nature of Satan came into the world that this whole planet changed. The Bible tells us that Creation groans even now in travail waiting for its deliverance. (Rom. 8:22.)

You may ask, "Does that mean we're not to eat meat?" No, I didn't say that. As the Bible tells us: **Every creature of God is good, and nothing to be refused, if it be received with thanksgiving: For it is sanctified by the word of God and prayer** (1 Tim. 4:4,5). Just make sure you sanctify it by God's Word and prayer before you consume it.

God's Day of Rest

Let's continue reading in the book of Genesis, chapter 2:

Thus the heavens and the earth were finished, and all the host of them.

And on the seventh day God ended his work which he had made; and he rested on the seventh day from all his work which he had made.

And God blessed the seventh day, and sanctified it: because that in it he had rested from all his work which God created and made.

Genesis 2:1-3

God blessed day seven as the day of rest and He sanctified it, or set it apart.

I remember as a kid how stores were closed on Sunday. The only jobs being operated on Sunday were those which provided things we needed in order to exist. Businesses were closed every Sunday out of respect to the Word of God. That's the way it was in this country until about thirty years ago.

God did not intend for man to work seven days a week. When people work that hard, their bodies can break down because they are stepping out of God's perfect will.

Wives should not be pushing their husbands to work seven days in order to pay the bills that they have accumulated. If they do that, they won't have their husbands for long. Neither should husbands be pushing their wives to be out working so hard. When either of them are forcing the other one to work like that, they are stepping out of God's plan and out of God's will.

As we see here in His Word, God never intended for His creation to work seven days a week. We were not made to do so. God blessed day seven as a day of rest. Believe it or not, everybody needs some rest — including you. If you don't take a rest, you could wind up in bad shape.

So God rested Himself after working for six days in the Creation:

> **And God blessed the seventh day, and sanctified it: because that in it he had rested from all his work which God created and made.**
>
> **Genesis 2:3**

Endnotes

[1]James Strong, "Hebrew and Chaldee Dictionary," in *Strong's Exhaustive Condordance of the Bible* (Nashville: Abingdon, 1890), p. 99, #6754.

[2]Strong, "Hebrew," p. 31, #1823.

[3]Merrill F. Unger, *The New Unger's Bible Dictionary*, (Chicago: Moody Bible Institute, 1957, 1985, 1988), p. 607.

[4]Strong, "Hebrew," p. 107, #7287.

2
Man's God-Given Authority Over the Earth

God spent six days creating this planet. As we have already seen, chapter 1 of Genesis gives the chronological account of what God did at the beginning in forming and creating, or re-creating, the earth from day one through day six. Chapter 2 of Genesis is not about the chronology. This chapter gives us specific information about things that happened on certain days.

Beginning with verse 4, it says:

> These are the generations of the heavens and of the earth when they were created, in the day that the Lord God made the earth and the heavens,
> And every plant of the field before it was in the earth, and every herb of the field before it grew: for the Lord God had not caused it to rain upon the earth, and there was not a man to till the ground.
>
> Genesis 2:4,5

When God had formed the field and every herb of the field, Scripture says, **There was not a man to till the ground.** In other words, the ground needed to be cultivated. I believe God had always intended for someone to be there to work that ground.

Continuing in chapter 2, we get another look at day six before God created man:

> But there went up a mist from the earth, and watered the whole face of the ground.
>
> Genesis 2:6

17

God took care of this planet by watering the ground with mist which came up from the earth. In effect, God had His own irrigation system. This occurred before rain ever existed. The first rain was not known about until the time of Noah. (See Gen. 6 and 7.)

The earth needed to be cared for, so what did God do about it?

God Created Man

And the Lord God formed man of the dust of the ground, and breathed into his nostrils the breath of life; and man became a living soul.

Genesis 2:7

This verse says, **And the Lord God** *formed* **man....** The word *formed* here means "to mold."[1] So this Scripture was saying:

And the Lord God *molded* **man of the dust of the ground, and breathed into his nostrils the breath of life; and man became a living soul.**

Now notice that man did not become a living soul until God had breathed into him the breath of life. God took His own life force and put it into man's physical body which He had made. The human body originally came from the dust of the ground, but it was God Who put life into it.

Life Begins in the Mother's Womb

Like every other human being, I have lived in a physical body for my entire life. Ten years ago, my body was a little smaller than it is today; twenty years ago, it was even smaller. But just because it was smaller did not make it any less my body. Thirty-nine years ago, my body was living inside my mother's womb. Though even much smaller then, it was still my body.

While in my mother's womb, I was the same person that I am today. My arms and legs are no different from those that were formed in my mother's womb, only now they are the size of an adult. I was growing the entire time I was inside the womb, and I continued to grow after I came out.

No one can look at me and dispute that this is my body and that it was my body when I was in my mother's womb. My body never belonged to my mother; I just happened to be living inside her. Her womb was the incubator God had provided for me. When I came out of the womb, my tiny body was placed in another incubator at the hospital so that I could be kept warm and secure.

As was mentioned previously, God fashioned the man and formed his physical body in the beginning, but that body could make no move until God had put life into it.

The same thing occurs between a man and a woman when they join physically in the sexual union. Their bodies, which were made of dust, come together to produce another body made of dust. Her egg joins together with his seed and a new body is created by their union. But nothing happens to that new body until life enters into it. It is God Who puts life into that new body, and no human being has the right to snuff it out through abortion or any other means.

The "Right to Choose" Movement

These days women are arguing about their right to choose. They say, "I have a right to do what I want with my own body."

That's absolutely true. Every woman can do what she wants with *her own body*. She has the right to choose what she will allow her body to experience, whether good or bad. In fact, as human beings, we all have that right regarding our bodies. But none of us have that right whenever our actions affect another person's body, whether that body is inside or outside the mother's womb.

A Garden Eastward in Eden

**And the Lord God planted a garden eastward in
Eden; and there he put the man whom he had formed.**
Genesis 2:8

This Garden of Eden must have been a massive place.
Verses 10-14 in chapter 2 of Genesis describe a river that ran
out of the garden in four different directions. Verse 13 tells
us that one of the lands it covered was Ethiopia, so we
know that the Garden of Eden covered part of the areas we
now know as Africa and the Middle East.

We don't know precisely where the first man and
woman lived, but we do know it was in that part of the
world.

Man's First Job

**And the Lord God took the man, and put him into
the garden of Eden to dress it and to keep it.**
Genesis 2:15

The Hebrew word for "dress" is *abad*, meaning "to
work, to serve, to till."[2] In other words, God looked and saw
that someone was needed to till or work the ground.

After forming man out of the ground, God gave him his
first assignment: to dress and keep the garden. That was the
first job man was given to do.

God's Order

Notice God gave man the responsibility of this job
before He made the woman. That's the proper order in life.
God gave man a choice.

The way I see it, a man has no business marrying a
woman until he has a job! If man is in God's plan and is
doing things God's way, then he will keep in God's order:
no job — no woman.

Any woman foolish enough to marry a man who is without a job is just that: a foolish woman who marries an unwise man.

No woman should be so unwise as to join herself to a man who isn't working and at the same time say, "We'll just live on love! We'll be poor together and raise ourselves up together." If that's what you have been saying, then you had better read the Bible and learn more about God's plan for man.

Remember, this first job was man's before the woman came along! It was God's intention for man to work. Now this was before the fall of man (which we will look into in a later chapter). The difference is, when God first told the man to dress the garden and to keep it, it was an easy job because that was before sin had come into the picture. Only after sin entered the world did man's job become hard work. There is always a heavy price to pay for sin.

First Work, Then Reward

I want you to notice something else in the plan of God:

And the Lord God took the man, and put him into the garden of Eden to dress it and to keep it.

And the Lord God commanded the man, saying, Of every tree of the garden thou mayest freely eat.
Genesis 2:15,16

God was saying to Adam: "Now you can have the fruit in this garden; but to get it you first have to work the garden by dressing it and keeping it. Then you can have the reward of the fruit it produces."

That's the way God's plan has always been: work and reward. God's system says, "First, you work; then you get the reward." God never intended for it to be reward without work. His plan is for His people to be rewarded through their work.

Our society should always be built upon work, with people being rewarded for it. Then there will be value and order. People will understand that, first, they must do certain things before they will be able to receive. It will be a society based upon solid principles.

This is the reason God is against gambling, whatever its form. Gambling is against God's plan for man.

When men can skip work and think based upon chance that they may win something that way, it breaks down the entire order of their society. When a society is based on anything other than work, its men and women take on the wrong attitudes, and children aren't being taught what their roles are. With this kind of thinking, people can get out of whack and walk away from the blessings of God. So forget about buying lottery tickets and stay away from the casinos. That was never God's plan.

God's plan is for His man to be healthy in every way, and a man can be truly healthy only when he has made his earnings by the sweat of his brow. That gives him a feeling of self-worth, which every man needs.

A Man Without a Job

God always has a job for man to do. A man without a job is an emaciated man. That's why a wife can see her husband change after he loses his job. Different guys react differently, but a man without a job is a man in trouble.

I'm for creating jobs for men, and women too. God wants them to have jobs, and they can. Every person should be doing something. If you don't have a job right now, then volunteer your time. Everyone needs to stay busy.

The worst thing is for a man to sit around doing nothing. Now sometimes things will happen and people will find themselves temporarily out of work. But I'm not talking about a temporary situation; I'm talking about a way of life.

No son should ever see his father just sitting around the house. The man of the household should get up, get dressed, go out and do something! A boy shouldn't come home from school every day and see his daddy sitting around with his feet propped up, drawing a check from the government that's being paid for by somebody else's work. That's wrong! It's not God's plan for man!

Welfare

I believe the worst thing that ever happened in our society was the welfare system.

As good-hearted as the intentions of welfare may have been, its results have been endemic. Welfare is absolutely contrary to Scripture. As we have already learned, God's original plan was twofold: work and reward.

Now the Bible talks about giving to the poor, about helping our brothers and sisters, about bearing one another's burdens. (Prov. 19:17; Matt. 25:40; Gal. 6:2.) But a segment of society or a system where people get rewarded without working is against God's plan.

This is why we have such a mess these days. People have decided, "I'm smarter than God so I'll just do things my own way." Then when they get the results, which surely will come to them eventually, they find out they aren't really as smart as God. The Bible says:

> **There is a way which seemeth right unto a man, but the end thereof are the ways of death.**
>
> **Proverbs 14:12**

This is what we have seen develop: a society that is laden with death.

Throughout this country there are men refusing to take the responsibility to be the father of the home. Many of them are being given money by our government for doing nothing. As a result, people are being destroyed. That was never God's will for man, and it's wrong!

Much of this is happening in the Church. People have forgotten what God said about a matter. They have based their lives on what they believe and have ordered their lives according to how they think. That's the problem. They have lived too much by what *they* think and not enough by what God says in His Word.

Working To Give

According to God's Word, it's good for men to work. A man without a job is a man with a problem. He can't be out of work for too long; he has to be doing something.

In the Old Testament, men had to work and labor with their own hands so that they would have something to eat. But the born-again Christian of the New Testament does not work to live; he works to give.

Notice Ephesians 4:28, which says:

> ...let him labour, working with his hands the thing which is good, that he may have to give to him that needeth.

Under the New Testament, the born-again believer is to labor with his hands that he may have to give to those in need. He works a job in order that he may have sustenance to take care of himself and his family. But he should not be looking at his job as his real source of supply. He must recognize the Lord as the Source of his supply and come to know for himself the truth of Philippians 4:19, which says:

> My God shall supply all your need according to his riches in glory by Christ Jesus.

Man's Choice

Let's go back now to God's instructions to Adam in the garden. God had told Adam he could eat of the tree of the garden as long as he worked the garden. Scripture says:

> **And the Lord God commanded the man, saying, Of every tree of the garden thou mayest freely eat.**
>
> **Genesis 2:16**

Then in verse 17 God said:

> **But of the tree of the knowledge of good and evil, thou shalt not eat of it: for in the day that thou eatest thereof thou shalt surely die.**

God gave man an opportunity to choose. He was saying to Adam: "There is a tree in the midst of the garden, but you are not to eat of it, because the day you eat it, you shall surely die." Notice God never said to him, "Don't touch it."

God's plan was always to give man a choice. God doesn't want a robot or an automaton; He wants a man who will follow Him because he has decided in his own heart that's what he wants to do.

God wants people to follow His will of their own volition, but they can't do that unless they have choice.

We can choose how we will live: either for God or for the devil.

As Ephesians 4:27 tells us: **Neither give place to the devil.**

This Scripture in *The Amplified Bible* says: **Leave no [such] room or foothold for the devil — give no opportunity to him.**

This verse is saying, "Don't give the devil an inch. Don't give him any ground." If you give him an inch, he will want ten country miles.

We can live in accordance with God's Word or against God's Word. We can do whatever we want and God will protect our right to do it. He will even protect our right to go to hell if we want to.

In the beginning God gave man this choice. God was saying to Adam, "You have a choice, but don't cross Me. If you do, you will pay the price for it."

God has always given each of us a choice. We have the right to choose concerning ourself, but we don't have any right to choose concerning somebody else.

Man's Next Job

God had some more work for Adam to do. He gave Adam a second job, and it was quite a job. The Scripture says:

> And out of the ground the Lord God formed every beast of the field, and every fowl of the air; and brought them unto Adam to see what he would call them: and whatsoever Adam called every living creature, that was the name thereof.
>
> **Genesis 2:19**

God brought to Adam every creature on the planet so that it could be named, and Adam named every beast, every bird, every insect. Just think about it: There are millions of insects alone.

God utilized man's marvelous capacity. The first man, Adam, was brilliant because the strong anointing of God was on him. He communed with God.

God had said to him, "You have dominion over the earth. I am bringing everything to you so that you will take control."

God intends for man to be in control. A man out of control is a man out of the will of God, but a man in control can be used by God.

Then we come to verse 20, which says:

> And Adam gave names to all cattle, and to the fowl of the air, and to every beast of the field....

Note what God had done to make every living creature: He formed each of them out of the ground — every beast of the field and every fowl of the air. Then He brought every living creature to Adam to see what he would call them, and Adam named each of them.

Adam had been doing his job, but something was missing. Note the rest of this verse:

> ...**but for Adam there was not found an help meet for him.**
>
> **Genesis 2:20**

Endnotes

[1]Strong, "Hebrew," p. 51, #3335.

[2]Strong, "Hebrew," p. 84, #5647.

3

Woman Made for Man

And the Lord God said, It is not good that the man should be alone; I will make him an help meet for him.

Genesis 2:18

This phrase *help meet* tells us a few things about a woman's responsibilities. Both words *help* and *meet* in this verse are from the Hebrew word which means "aid."[1]

God was saying, "It's not good for man to be alone, so I will make an aid for him."

It isn't good for man to be alone; he needs a woman — but only *one* woman.

Notice God didn't say that He would make *helps* — plural — for man and that all of them would be adaptable and suitable for him. It was never God's plan for one man to have multiple women.

God said, "I will make a help for man." That's singular! God meant for there to be one woman for one man.

Taken From Adam's Rib

As we saw, Adam had worked to name all the animals in the garden. Then he realized that there still was no one for him. He didn't as yet have what he really needed: *an help meet for him.*

And the Lord God caused a deep sleep to fall upon Adam, and he slept: and he took one of his ribs, and closed up the flesh instead thereof;

And the rib, which the Lord God had taken from man, made he a woman, and brought her unto the man.

And Adam said, This is now bone of my bones, and flesh of my flesh: she shall be called Woman, because she was taken out of Man.

Genesis 2:21-23

As mentioned previously, God had formed man out of the dust of the earth. He reached down into the dirt, took some clay and formed the man.

But when it came to the creation of the woman, this was different. She was specially made by God.

In verse 22 the Hebrew word translated *made* means "to build."[2]

God caused the man to sleep, then He took a rib out of man's side and from it built, crafted and created for him a special creature. She was fashioned and specially designed by God. Then God **brought her unto the man** (v. 22).

Ladies, note that God presented her to him, so let Him do it for you; instead of you presenting yourself.

Let me tell you how I think it all happened when God brought this wonderful creation to Adam. When Adam woke up, God said, "Adam, I have something for you." Then Adam saw what the Lord had created from within his own body. When he looked around and saw all the other creatures God had made, he realized what a special prize he had received from God.

God's Crowning Creation

Remember it was Adam's responsibility to name everything. So when he saw this new creature, he said, **She shall be called Woman, because she was taken out of Man** (v. 23). In other words, she was "man with a womb." That's what a woman is.

Woman is God's crowning creation. She is the mother of all things. She was built by God to be admired by man. She was not made to be hit or thrown down or handled roughly. She was made to be handled delicately.

Man and Woman as One

Therefore shall a man leave his father and his mother, and shall cleave unto his wife: and they shall be one flesh.

Genesis 2:24

We are talking here about God's plan for man in the beginning.

God did not allow the first man to have this beautiful creature as a helpmate until he was ready to receive her. Adam had been doing his job and he had a feeling of his own worth. He was ready to take upon himself that which had been specially crafted for him by God. I believe this is God's will for every man who is seeking a successful marriage.

Each man needs to realize that there is a woman who has been especially crafted and built to fit him. The husband should see his wife as God's gift to him; the single man should be believing God for just the right woman to be his mate.

God's plan is for the woman, as man's helpmate, to be adapting and completing to him.

This is different from the women's lib attitude in which a woman says, "I'm my own person. I don't need a man to tell me anything. I'm an independent woman." There is a place for being independent; I don't disagree with that. But I'm talking here about God's plan. I know society may say something different, but we need to know what the Bible says.

The woman's role is to become one with the man and to adapt her life to his. God made her for that purpose. By adapting to him she helps to round out his life, and he needs that. And because God created woman to also be fulfilled, she will find fulfillment in being a completion to her godly man.

The man who is alone doesn't have everything; he can't do or know it all, and he can't be everywhere. When he is lacking, the woman as his wife will help to fill that void. She will be for him what he is not. She will help him be all that he can be; that is, if he's smart enough to let her. A smart man will allow his woman to do that.

Men ought to learn to listen to their wives, and wives ought to take up their rightful role without trying to run the lives of their men. No woman should be standing toe to toe and nose to nose with her husband, saying, "You're not my daddy!" No, he isn't her daddy. But as her husband, she should be seeing him in a role that is higher than her daddy.

Gift of Singleness

Let's look at this Scripture again:

And the Lord God said, It is not good that the man should be alone; I will make him an help meet for him.
Genesis 2:18

Now I want you to note what God says here: **It is not good that the man should be alone**.

There are, however, certain exceptions to this. God has given some people the gift of singleness. These individuals have been called by God to be eunuchs for the kingdom of God's sake in order to minister the Gospel.

But when I found out I didn't have this gift of singleness, I had to do something about it.

Now this doesn't mean if you are single that you can't take care of yourself and keep yourself walking holy before the Lord, especially concerning sex. You *can* — by acting on the Word of God.

But it isn't good for a man to be without a wife, unless called by God to be alone. Every man needs a wife, but marriage must come to him in time and in proper order — when he has matured a little, when he knows who he is, when he has a job and can support a wife. No man should take on the responsibility of a wife before he has gotten his own act together.

Except for those whom the Lord has spoken to and called to celibacy, every man needs a wife. No man is really complete without one. And I have news for every single man: God has one out there just for you.

Now if you say God has not given you the gift of singleness but after decades you haven't found a woman, something may be wrong. It's possible that you may have a problem and need deliverance. If you have an attraction to the same sex, God can deliver you from it. I have been all around the country and seen people delivered from that demonic oppression.

But don't get me wrong. I'm not saying every guy who has been single for quite a while has anything wrong with him. A person can be single a long time and still live holy before God. He can still be looking for the right woman to share his life while he works to get his own self together. But he needs to choose correctly.

The Word says of the man, **Whoso findeth a wife findeth a good thing, and obtaineth favour of the Lord** (Prov. 18:22).

In describing the virtuous woman, the Word says, **Her children arise up, and call her blessed; her husband also, and he praiseth her** (Prov. 31:28).

God is pleased when a man and woman choose to come together as husband and wife.

I realize we are living in "the modern era" when people "don't have to be married anymore." But those who choose to live together really aren't trying to follow God's plan.

The reason we have so much chaos, so much poverty and so many problems these days is because men have moved away from God's plan for their lives. If a man will follow God's plan, then blessings will come. But by following his own plans and feeding his own sexual desires, he will get himself into trouble.

Man's Spiritual Place

Men are supposed to be the ones who spend time before God and hear from the Lord. Then they are to communicate to their families, "Thus saith the Lord...."

God wants to communicate with men, and He will if they will spend enough time with Him. But too often men have transferred the spiritual responsibilities to the women. For this reason, boys grow up in the home thinking it's somehow sissified to love God and spend time with Him and listen to Him. They see all that as "women's stuff."

One of the things I'm so proud of about my church is that there are as many men involved as there are women.

So there is nothing sissified about being saved! In fact, it takes a real man to be saved and make the decision to live right before God and man.

Any animal formed out of the dust of the ground can follow the desires of the loins. No one needs a special appetite to make that decision. But it takes a real man to decide that there is a right way and a wrong way.

The husband should be hearing from God about what he is to do. He isn't supposed to just do whatever he decides. He needs to hear what God has to say. He should spend time before the Lord and find out what God wants for him and his family.

Any man who is stumbling around, messing up and blowing money here and there is just following his own pride. As long as he refuses to listen to God, he will keep making mistakes and causing life to be tough on his family.

The husband's role is to hear what God has to say, but he has to spend time before God to do it. He can't be leading his family in the right direction unless he has listened to the Leader.

Woman's Role Is to Adapt

Adam communicated God's instructions to the woman in the garden. That's the only way she could have found out about it. There is no record that God said anything to her since she wasn't there.

Genesis 2:16,17 says:

> **And the Lord God commanded *the man*, saying, Of every tree of the garden thou mayest freely eat:**
>
> **But of the tree of the knowledge of good and evil, thou shalt not eat of it: for in the day that thou eatest thereof thou shalt surely die.**

Woman wasn't created yet because the next verse says:

> **And the Lord God said, It is not good that the man should be alone; I will make him an help meet for him (v. 18).**

So we see from these verses that Adam had to have communicated to his wife what the Lord had said they were to do.

Before I met my wife, God had told me I would be in the ministry. He spoke to me about it, and I knew what He had said. Then Deborah came into my life and we were joined to one another in marriage.

After that, the Lord called me into full-time ministry, and He let me know exactly what He wanted me to do. So I said to Deborah, "The Lord has told me what we are to do."

It was Deborah's responsibility as my wife to adapt herself to God's instructions, and she did. She said, "If that's what the Lord has said, then that's what we have to do."

Deborah entered Bible school with me, and we graduated together. She was pregnant while we attended the Bible school, but that didn't stop her. Since there were no elevators in the school at that time, she just waddled up and down those stairs while carrying the baby.

As a wife, Deborah wanted to adapt herself to her husband. She wanted to understand what I was doing, where I was coming from, why I made the decisions that I did. She wanted to understand who I was so that she would be able to fulfill her role as my wife, and thereby fulfill God's will for her life too.

I know for a fact that, if I had been married to a woman who did not feel as Deborah did, I probably would not be here today doing the will of God in my life.

At that time there was a whole group of young preachers who were close to my age. Today only a handful of them are even in the ministry. Why? Because their wives could not adapt themselves to God's call. Some of those men didn't accept a call to preach until after they were married, but their wives simply said, "I didn't marry a preacher!"

Wives, what if God calls the man you are married to? If that happens, you will have to adapt yourself to his calling. You can't say, "But I didn't marry a preacher." The truth is, you have married whatever person your husband turns out to be. This may not be popular teaching, but it's still the truth.

God's Order of Responsibility

But I would have you know, that the head of every man is Christ; and the head of the woman is the man; and the head of Christ is God.

1 Corinthians 11:3

Christ is the Head of every man. God's order is for the man to be the most spiritual person in his home. He is to pray, spend time in God's Word, find out God's will for his family and then tell them what God has said. As husband and father, he is to be the best example he can be of that kind of life.

After having received the orders of Christ, any man who is not functioning accordingly is out of the will of God.

For the man is not of the woman; but the woman of the man.

Neither was the man created for the woman; but the woman for the man.

For this cause ought the woman to have power on her head because of the angels.

1 Corinthians 11:8-10

The word *power* here in verse 10 means "covering" according to *The Amplified Bible*.

In some churches, women wear a veil or a hat on their heads to signify that they are in subjection to their husband. This was the custom in early Church days.

Nevertheless neither is the man without the woman, neither the woman without the man, in the Lord.

For as the woman is of the man, even so is the man also by the woman; but all things of God.

1 Corinthians 11:11,12

In other words, this is saying the man is to work with the woman but not dominate her. He is of her and she is of him. But God does have an order.

The head of Christ is God the Father. So God's order is, first, the Father, then the Son and then the man in the home.

Fatherless Homes

A home without a man is a home that is absolutely out of whack. God did not intend for the woman to be head of the household. But there are times when situations occur which cause a woman to be thrust into the headship of her house. That can happen because of a death or some other circumstance.

In such a predicament the woman does the very best that she can. It's tough for her to have to fulfill the roles of both mother and father to her family. A woman having both jobs deserves all the help she can get.

God's plan for man was that there be no fatherless homes. But unfortunately these days too many such situations have occurred. As a result, there is no example of leadership for the young man to follow.

We are seeing babies having babies in fatherless homes. When that happens, boys grow up without any example of leadership from another man in their home. The girl doesn't find out what her role is to be and the boy never learns what his role is. Everything gets out of line, and very often people wind up on some kind of public assistance. The entire order of things has become confused and distorted.

No wonder then there is chaos among the people. One reason we have so much crime in the streets is because people have forgotten about the Bible. Too many pastors and church leaders are spending time preaching to their people about politics, civil rights and other situations. There is a place for all of that, but not from the pulpit. When you go to church, you should be fed God's Word and what it says.

Endnotes

[1]Strong, "Hebrew," p. 668, #5828.

[2]Strong, "Hebrew," p. 22, #1129.

4

Authority Given Over to Satan

> Now the serpent was more subtil than any beast of
> the field which the Lord God had made. And he said
> unto the woman, Yea, hath God said, Ye shall not eat of
> every tree of the garden?
>
> **Genesis 3:1**

Here we see Satan using the serpent to question the
woman about God's commandment. As previously
mentioned, Satan was on this planet before man was
created. After going into combat against God, Satan [then
called Lucifer] and a third of the angels following him were
cast out of heaven and down to the earth.

"Hath God Said...?"

Notice that after entering into the serpent, Satan speaks
to the woman, not the man. He says to her:

> Yea, hath God said, Ye shall not eat of every tree of
> the garden? (v. 1).

He was questioning whether God really said that and if
He really meant it. Satan's tactics still have not changed.

The Woman's Response

> And the woman said unto the serpent, We may eat
> of the fruit of the trees of the garden.
>
> **Genesis 3:2**

The woman answered him by saying, *We may eat....*
What does this mean? She was correctly speaking about
both of them in their marriage.

In marriage today, there seems to be too much use of the words, *I, me* and *my*. Married people are always saying things like, "*I* want it," "Do it for *me*, "This is *my* car." These two people are acting as though they were single. To them it's *his* money and *her* money, *his* car and *her* car.

But that's not the way marriage is supposed to be. The husband and wife are to be as one — in name, aim, purpose, thought and direction.

The problem is, so many folks come to the marriage union still wanting to act single while enjoying the fruit of sex. They want the sexual union without everything that goes along with it. But both husband and wife must give up their autonomy when they get married. It's no longer one person always saying, "Let's do what *I* want when *I* want it." There must come a time of negotiation.

If you are not willing to negotiate with a spouse, then don't ever get married, because you are not yet mature enough for marriage. Maturity means more than just age. You can be forty years old and still not be mature.

> **And the woman said unto the serpent, We may eat of the fruit of the trees of the garden:**
> **But of the fruit of the tree which is in the midst of the garden, God hath said, Ye shall not eat of it, neither shall ye touch it, lest ye die.**
>
> **Genesis 3:2,3**

Now the woman wasn't around when God made His first commandment to man. That's when God told Adam what he could and could not do in the garden:

> **...Of every tree of the garden thou mayest freely eat:**
> **But of the tree of the knowledge of good and evil, thou shalt not eat of it: for in the day that thou eatest thereof thou shalt surely die.**
>
> **Genesis 2:16,17**

Since the woman wasn't around then, how did she find out about it? Through God's order of things. There was to be communication. Adam communicated with his wife, telling her what the Lord had said.

Satan Appeals to Her Instinct

> And the woman said unto the serpent, We may eat of the fruit of the trees of the garden:

> But of the fruit of the tree which is in the midst of the garden, God hath said, Ye shall not eat of it, neither shall ye touch it, lest ye die.

> And the serpent said unto the woman, Ye shall not surely die.

> **Genesis 3:2-4**

Today it is still Satan's tactic to say, "No, that's not what God really said."

> And the serpent said unto the woman, Ye shall not surely die.

> For God doth know that in the day ye eat thereof, then your eyes shall be opened, and ye shall be as gods, knowing good and evil.

> And when the woman saw that the tree was good for food, and that it was pleasant to the eyes, and a tree to be desired to make one wise, she took of the fruit thereof, and did eat, and gave also unto her husband with her; and he did eat.

> **Genesis 3:4-6**

The serpent appealed to the woman's desire for more. She saw the tree and it was pleasant to her eyes.

What does the word *pleasant* mean? In the Hebrew it means it was desirable;[1] in other words, it was pretty. As we know, women like pretty things.

Let me give you an example. One time at our church in Philadelphia, my wife was given a bouquet of long-stemmed yellow roses. She looked at them and said, "Oh, how beautiful!" Now had I been given a bouquet like that, I would have simply said, "Thank you."

Before meeting Deborah, I was dating another girl and I bought her some flowers. I remember how she cried over them, saying, "Oh, they're so pretty!" She put them in a vase and kept smelling them and looking at them. She just loved them!

Then one day she sent me a gift: it was flowers! I thought, *What are these for?!* Flowers might be pretty, but they just didn't have the same effect on me as they had on her.

For some reason a woman will do something like that for a man, but she doesn't really understand. What she feels and sees and appreciates about something is quite different from the way a man will react to it. He doesn't respond to the same stimuli.

When a dozen roses are handed to a woman, she loves it because she sees how pretty they are. But if a guy gets them, he just feels awkward. It doesn't even look right when a man is holding a bouquet of flowers in his hands. To me, there's something wrong with that picture. He would probably drop them in the first trash basket he found. Women can see how pretty things like that are, but most men just aren't geared that way. They see things differently.

So Satan appealed to the woman's natural instinct. To her, **...it was pleasant to the eyes, and a tree to be desired to make one wise** (Gen. 3:6).

The Man Heard It All, But Said Nothing!

So what did the woman do?

> **...she took of the fruit thereof, and did eat, and *gave also unto her husband with her*; and he did eat.**
> **Genesis 3:6**

Here we see a man unwilling to stand in his rightful place of authority. Adam was with the woman when all this had happened. He heard the serpent say words different from what God had said, but not once did he challenge those words.

Adam could have told the serpent: "Shut your mouth! God told me I have authority over you, so get out of here! And don't you ever speak to that woman again!"

The serpent would have had to obey Adam instantly, because God had given Adam dominion. But Adam didn't say a thing.

She Was Deceived, But He Was Not

Now the woman had gotten out of order. She was leading Adam, saying to him, "Here — you eat some of this fruit." She was deceived because of what she could see with her eyes.

But Adam was not deceived. He understood what was going on. He was standing there while all of this had occurred between the woman and the serpent, but he failed to take his rightful place of authority.

So he ate the fruit of that tree; and when he did, both of them died spiritually. They stepped out of the will of God, out of God's order for man. God has an order for everything; He knows what He is doing.

After they had sinned, they were sentenced by the Lord with punishments for their unwillingness to abide by His commandment. (We will discuss these punishments in a later chapter.)

As a result of their disobedience, the Scripture says:

> **And the Lord God said, Behold, the man is become as one of us, to know good and evil: and now, lest he put forth his hand, and take also of the tree of life, and eat, and live for ever.**
>
> **Genesis 3:22**

Then the Word tells us they were banished from the Garden of Eden:

> **Therefore the Lord God sent him forth from the garden of Eden, to till the ground from whence he was taken.**
>
> **So he drove out the man; and he placed at the east of the garden of Eden Cherubims, and a flaming sword which turned every way, to keep the way of the tree of life.**
>
> **Genesis 3:23,24**

Had fallen man been able to partake of the Tree of Life, he would have then entered into his eternal state, and there would have been no hope for his redemption.

So God drove them out of the Garden of Eden and placed cherubims at the entrance of the garden, with a flaming sword to keep man from entering into the garden again.

Endnote

[1]*The Holy Bible, King James Version.* (Camden, NJ: Thomas Nelson, 1972), p. 3, footnote #2.

5
Satan's Devices

I want us to look again in Genesis, chapter 3, at some of Satan's devices in his attempt to destroy man. He is still using these same tactics today to get at unsuspecting mankind who are trying to follow and serve God. As the apostle Paul said, we are not to be ignorant of Satan's devices. (2 Cor. 2:11.)

The Word of God tells us that people can be drawn away and enticed. (James 1:14.) Satan always comes and challenges what God has said, as he did with the woman, saying to her, "Did God really say this?"

Now the serpent was more subtil than any beast of the field which the Lord God had made. And he said unto the woman, Yea, hath God said, Ye shall not eat of every tree of the garden?

And the woman said unto the serpent, We may eat of the fruit of the trees of the garden:

But of the fruit of the tree which is in the midst of the garden, God hath said, Ye shall not eat of it, neither shall ye touch it, lest ye die.

And the serpent said unto the woman, Ye shall not surely die:

For God doth know that in the day ye eat thereof, then your eyes shall be opened, and ye shall be as gods, knowing good and evil.

And when the woman saw that the tree was good for food, and that it was pleasant to the eyes, and a tree to be desired to make one wise, she took of the fruit thereof, and did eat, and gave also unto her husband with her; and he did eat.

Genesis 3:1-6

Remember the woman found out from her husband what God had said. She wasn't there when God had said it, because she hadn't been created yet. So Adam told her about it. That's called communication. There is supposed to be communication between a husband and his wife.

Now you may say, "But I just can't talk to people." Then you don't need to get married yet. It's time you came out of your shell. You have to be willing to communicate and make yourself vulnerable to another person. That means you have to start talking — period.

The only way two married people can form a bond and really get things done is by communicating with one another.

God had said to Adam, **Of the tree of the knowledge of good and evil, thou shalt not eat of it...** (Gen. 2:17). God didn't tell him not to touch it; He just said, **Thou shalt not eat of it.**

But when Adam talked to the woman, from what she said we can see he told her two things about what God had said:

We may eat of the fruit of the trees of the garden:

But of the fruit of the tree which is in the midst of the garden, God hath said, *Ye shall not eat of it, neither shall ye touch it*, lest ye die.

Genesis 3:2,3

She was telling the serpent what Adam had told her. Now these words, **...neither shall ye touch it...**, were Adam's addition. He had said to her, "Not only are we not to eat it, we are not even to touch it, lest we die."

Now I want you to notice Satan's approach. The first thing he did was to come and challenge what God had said. There are some avenues Satan takes to try and stop people from fulfilling God's will for their lives. Let's consider some of the ways in which he operates.

Challenging What the Lord Says

Satan is always asking questions like, "Is that *really* what the Bible says? Is that *really* what it means?"

That's where Satan comes from with the idea of evolution. As mentioned previously, science and the Bible do not necessarily contradict one another, because clearly there was something here on this earth before Adam and Eve. The evidence points to there having been a prehistoric age with all those dinosaurs. However, no evidence points to humans being derived from some other animal like a monkey or a fish.

The Bible tells us that in the beginning all of those animals came from the same place: God created them out of the dust of the ground. But He created, or formed, the man in His image. That's where science and the Word go in different directions. Something occurred in this planet through time; but where man is concerned, there was no change. We have found not one human being that was half-horse or half-fish or half-monkey.

The first thing the serpent did with the woman was to challenge what God had said. He questioned her by asking, **Yea, hath God said...?** (v. 1).

This is what Satan continually does. He tries to challenge what God has said in His Word. He questions the believer, saying, "If you are really healed, then how come...? If God really provides for your needs, then how come...?"

Appealing to Lust

The next thing Satan did in the garden was to appeal to the woman's lust. Notice what he said to her in verse 5:

> **For God doth know that in the day ye eat thereof, then your eyes shall be opened, and ye shall be as gods, knowing good and evil.**

The devil was appealing to her lust of having control, and he is doing the same thing today. Now I'm not referring just to the woman of today; Satan deals this way with all of mankind. People have a lust to be their own god.

That's what humanism is all about. It says, "We don't need any God; we are our own god." This kind of teaching can be found in today's universities, and humanism is a religion.

When people push for the separation of church and state, they are meaning the separation of state and Christianity. Humanism is a religion that is being taught every day in universities. I know; I graduated from a university and I heard it for myself.

Satan appeals to the lust of people being their own god and doing things their own way — without Almighty God. If you are your own god, then you know good and evil, and you can decide to do whatever you want.

In the epistle of James, it is laid out for us just how Satan does this. In chapter 1 it says:

> **Blessed is the man that endureth temptation: for when he is tried, he shall receive the crown of life, which the Lord hath promised to them that love him.**
>
> **Let no man say when he is tempted, I am tempted of God: for God cannot be tempted with evil, neither tempteth he any man:**
>
> **But every man is tempted, when he is drawn away of his own lust, and enticed.**
>
> **James 1:12-14**

Satan tries to find out what appeals to you so that he can use it against you.

It might be your intellect or it might be education. There is nothing wrong with either of these, but you have to watch and keep them in their proper perspective.

What appeals to you might be power or money or attention or fame. Just as he did with the woman in the garden, Satan will say to you, "Oh, God doesn't want you to have that. He knows if you get it, you'll be...." He will try anything he can to find something that will draw you away and entice you.

Note James 1:15:

Then when lust hath conceived, it bringeth forth sin: and sin, when it is finished, bringeth forth death.

That means if you don't put a stop to that lust when Satan brings it to you, it will conceive. Then lust, when it has conceived, will bring forth sin; and sin, when it is finished, will bring forth death.

Lust. That's what Satan was doing with the woman in Genesis: he came and enticed her. Lust, if not checked, will cause you to fall into sin just as it did with her. Let's go back to Genesis, chapter 3, and look at this again. The serpent, talking to her, said:

For God doth know that in the day ye eat thereof, then your eyes shall be opened, and ye shall be as gods, knowing good and evil.

And when the woman *saw* that the tree was good for food....

Genesis 3:5,6

I don't believe she had even noticed this tree before. She had been in the garden all that time with her man, but do you know what she saw? Her man.

Satan had to point out this tree to her. That's what he does.

Bringing Attention to the Forbidden

And when the woman *saw* that the tree was good for food....

The woman paid attention to what was forbidden. Immediately she saw that it was desirable and pretty.

Paying attention to what Satan offers you will get you into trouble every time.

The enemy, Satan, wants you to pay attention to that which is forbidden. He will try to get you to look at it, meditate on it and think about it. If you don't reject it then and there, but just keep on thinking about it, you will fall into a snare.

When a man keeps looking at a woman with the feelings of desire in his heart, he will be enticed. Now the Bible does not say that just looking on a woman is sin; but as Jesus said, **Whosoever looketh on a woman to** *lust after her* **hath committed adultery with her already in his heart** (Matt. 5:28).

Something Pleasant to the Sight

When the woman *saw* **that the tree was good for food, and that it was pleasant to the** *eyes***, and a tree to be desired to make one wise....**

Genesis 3:6

She paid attention to the forbidden fruit, and when she did, she saw that it was desirable. It was something pretty for her to look at.

The enemy, Satan, will always approach us at our weakest link. If the devil had seen Adam as the weak one, he would have moved through him. But in this case the woman was the weak one, so he moved through her. He came at her by approaching an area that was natural for women, because women like things that are pretty.

Something That Feels Good

When the woman saw that the tree was good for food, and that it was pleasant to the eyes, and a tree to be desired to make one wise, she *took of the fruit* **thereof.**

Genesis 3:6

Then the woman *touched* the fruit. She put her hands on it.

So be challenged. There will be an appeal to your lusts. First, you will look, then you will listen, then you will touch.

Now I'm not just talking about sex here. I'm not even talking about the relationship between men and women. Satan can use anything — basketball, sewing, education, food or anything that's good — to pry you away from God. He will use whatever he can to take precedence over what God has said in His Word.

When your desire or interest for a certain thing is soaking up your time and attention, Satan will use it to try and drive a wedge between you and God.

So the serpent got the woman to touch that fruit. Now her husband had told her God had said, "Don't touch it." But remember, God never said that. When she touched the fruit, her senses were totally involved. She liked what she heard, what she saw and what she felt.

Whenever you touch the forbidden — anything that doesn't belong to you — it will cause you to be enticed. That's how Satan will come at you to break you away from the plan of God.

Partaking of the Forbidden

...she took of the fruit thereof, and did eat, and gave also unto her husband with her; and he did eat.

Genesis 3:6

First, she *touched* the forbidden; then she *partook* of it.

Touching it will cause you to partake of it. Then when you partake of it, the door is opened for sin. Whenever you step out and do something that is forbidden, Satan will work at causing you to pass it on to somebody else.

Satan is the author of venereal disease, which came about because of sin and unlawful acts against the Word of God. An example of this would be men involving themselves with bestiality. In writing the Law through Moses, God had to speak specifically against people who were having sex with animals and, as a result, had picked up diseases. After sin came along, the effects of that sin were passed along to others.

When you get over into sin, Satan will always try to convince you to become involved with somebody else. That's what happens with venereal diseases, as they are passed on to others.

Passing It to Others

When the woman ate of the fruit, she died spiritually. Then she passed some of it to her husband. When he ate of it, he died spiritually.

That's the way Satan always works through sin. Sin will entice you and hurt you, yet its effect will cause you to pass it on to someone else.

When the woman took that fruit, Adam was standing right there with her. All that time, he had heard what Satan was saying through the serpent. He heard God being challenged. He saw that the woman was interested. He heard what she said and saw what she did. At any point he could have put a stop to it.

But what we are seeing is a man who failed to live up to his responsibilities. As the head of his wife, Adam had been given the responsibility to protect her. The woman was made to be protected and looked after by him.

Adam was there when it all happened, but he did nothing. She was out of order and he was out of order. That's when the enemy, Satan, was able to come into the situation. When allowed to move into people's lives, he will come in like an eighteen-wheeler and roll everybody over.

The Result Was Death

God had said, **...in the day that thou eatest thereof** [of this tree] **thou shalt surely die** (Gen. 2:17). So that which God had said would happen actually took place.

Now let's look in First Timothy, chapter 2. I find this Scripture to be rather enlightening on the subject of what happened in that particular incident in the garden. The woman allowed herself to be tricked by the devil; but as the Word tells us, Adam was not deceived.

For Adam was first formed, then Eve.

And Adam was not deceived, but the woman being deceived was in the transgression.

1 Timothy 2:13,14

The woman was deceived, but she got deceived because she listened. She should have said to the serpent, "No, God and my husband have said...." Instead, she listened to the serpent and let him lead her off in the wrong direction.

She allowed lust to grab onto her. She allowed her eyes to cause her to be enticed. Then after touching the fruit, she said, "This is all right to the touch."

But she was tricked. One meaning of the word *trick* is to deceive. Satan is the deceiver of all mankind.

The woman was deceived, but this Scripture from First Timothy tells us that Adam was not deceived. He understood what was happening. He knew what was going on. He heard it all. He was there with the female Adam — the woman.

Adam's Choice

...she took of the fruit thereof, and did eat, and gave also unto her husband with her; and he did eat.

Genesis 3:6

So Adam was faced with a choice again.

He passed the initial test which came before the woman had been created. God had said to him, "Because you have done the work, you can partake of the fruit of every tree in this garden except for one." So Adam didn't touch that fruit. He was obedient to God's command.

Then the woman was created, or built, for him. Satan saw that he couldn't get through to the man, so he tried to entice the woman and was successful.

Adam, understanding what was going on in this situation, had another point of choice: whether he would allow another person to be put ahead of God. When the woman reached to touch that fruit, he should have stopped her. He should have said, "Don't touch it!" But he didn't say a word.

The woman listened to the devil and was tricked by what she heard him saying to her. Eventually he caused her to become disoriented; she was beguiled by him. Being deceived, she grabbed the fruit and ate it.

But Adam was not deceived. When the woman ate the fruit and then offered it to him, he could have said to her: "I told you not to eat of it, but you did it anyway. I don't know what's going to happen to you now. But I can't eat it because God said not to. I don't even want to touch it. So don't give it to me."

Adam knew all the time what was going on, and he had a choice. It was his decision about which way he would go. But he made a big mistake, the same mistake men and women are making, even years later: choosing women or men over God, choosing fame above everything else, caring more about what people think than what God has said.

I can tell you exactly what happened to Adam at that moment. They had been living in the glory of God; so when the woman partook of that forbidden fruit, the glory of God left her. Immediately Adam could see a difference. Then she held it out there in front of him, as if to say, "Come be with me."

Adam kept looking at her and thinking about what God had said. The fact is, he remembered what God had said. She was tricked, but he was not. In effect, she kept saying to him, "Come on — it's all right."

Then he said, "Give it to me!"

When he took it, he plunged into disobedience with her; and, like her, he died instantly.

They didn't die physically, but spiritually. In effect, they had fallen from grace. Before dying physically, Adam lived 930 years and fathered children upon children upon children.

Adam and Eve's son Cain killed his brother Abel, but it took Satan more than 900 years to find other ways to kill man. What took him 930 years to find a way to kill the first man, now takes only 70 or 80 years. He keeps working at it by filling mankind with care and worry and fear by which they can destroy themselves.

6
Man's Accountability

In the beginning man made the decision to put the woman ahead of God. Adam remembered what God had said to him, but he looked at the woman and chose her over God — and he paid the price for it.

Today men are doing the same thing. They seem so concerned about their fleshly needs and desires. They care more about some woman than they do about God. Just as Adam died spiritually because of it, so will they.

Put God First

God will have no other god before Him. That was the first of the Ten Commandments from God to the children of Israel. (See Ex. 20:3.)

You are not to allow any person — man or woman, boy or girl — to take precedence over the Lord God Himself in your life.

You cannot afford to put anybody or anything, even friendship, above God. It's better for you to be alone and with God. That, of course, is an oxymoron, because you can never be with God and be alone. However, for the sake of discussion, let me say it's better that you be alone and with God than to have all your friends, whether girlfriends or boyfriends. It's better to be with God by yourself and to be pure, having His anointing and His glory, than to have all the pleasures of sin for a season!

Never Put Blessings Ahead of God

God gave the woman to the man in order to bless him.

Whenever God has blessed you with money or position, don't turn around and cut your own neck by putting what God has given you ahead of Him. If you do, God will be unable to bless you, even in your giving.

The question is not, can God get it *to* you; but, can God get it *through* you?

You can't be holding on to what God has given you. You have to handle it like a loose garment. You have to say: "God, as far as I'm concerned, this is only on loan or lease; it's Yours anyway. If You say, 'Do it,' then I will do it. If You say, 'Go,' then I will go. If You say, 'Let go,' then I will let go. If You say, 'Hold on,' then I will hold on. I will do whatever You say for me to do."

Three Types of Death

Before we go any further in this study, let's look at the three types of death that are spoken of in the Bible.

Physical Death

There is physical death, which occurs when a person leaves his physical body.

Remember, though, your physical body is not the real you, but only the "house" in which you live. I can look at your "house" through the windows of my "house," the eyes.

When you leave this body, you will go somewhere. Now I'm going to heaven, and I hope that's where you go, but that is dependent upon your decision to make Jesus the Lord of your life. Once you have made that decision, then you will live for God and not the devil.

Spiritual Death

Then there is spiritual death. This is what God was talking about when He said to Adam, **...in the day that**

thou eatest thereof [of that tree] **thou shalt surely die** (Gen. 2:17).

Spiritual death has a twofold definition.

First, it means to be separated from God. The fellowship between God and Adam (both the male Adam and the female Adam) was broken because of sin.

Secondly, spiritual death is receiving Satan's nature, which is exactly what happened to Adam. The man and woman in the garden received the nature of the enemy, Satan, and that satanic nature showed up immediately in their children with their oldest son killing his brother.

Satan's nature is to kill, to steal and to destroy; God's nature is to give life. (John 10:10.) Satan's nature is based on fear; God's nature is based on faith. (1 John 4:17,18; 5:4.)

Eternal Death

Then there is eternal death. We find this in Revelation 20:14, which says that death and hell will be cast into the lake of fire. Hell is not the final place; it will be tossed into the lake of fire that will burn forever.

Effects of Sin

Now as we read in Scripture, Adam (both male and female) experienced spiritual death immediately. Its ramifications showed up in Genesis, chapter 3, as they heard the voice of God Who was walking in the cool of the day.

Fear

> **And the Lord God called unto Adam, and said unto him, Where art thou?**
>
> **Genesis 3:9**

Adam said:

> **I heard thy voice in the garden, and I was afraid...** (v. 10).

There was no fear in this planet until then. Adam had no knowledge of fear until after he had died spiritually.

Shame

As the Word tells us in Genesis 3, verse 7:

And the eyes of them both were opened, and they knew that they were naked....

For the first time Adam and his wife recognized that they were naked. They could see each other's bodies.

When Adam had first seen the woman, he had said, **This is bone of my bones, and flesh of my flesh: she shall be called Woman, because she was taken out of Man** (Gen. 2:23). He had noticed then that she had a body, but there was no shame in it. As Scripture says, **And they were both naked, the man and his wife, and were not ashamed** (v. 25).

Their bodies were basking in the light of God's glory. Not only were they physically beautiful, they were shining in His glory. But when they sinned, His glory departed from them. Then the Word tells us what happened when they noticed that they were naked:

The eyes of them both were opened, and they knew that they were naked; and they sewed fig leaves together, and made themselves aprons.

Genesis 3:7

Man Held Accountable

For as in Adam all die, even so in Christ shall all be made alive.

1 Corinthians 15:22

God held Adam accountable for the sin and death that came into the world. And that's the way it is.

In the same way God holds the man accountable for what happens in his marriage. It's the man's responsibility to keep wooing the woman, chasing after her and winning her, then cleaving to her and ministering to her as her husband. He is to work at keeping her happy, and she is to adapt herself to him and be complete for him.

The only real argument a husband and wife should be having is about which one will be a greater blessing to the other. That sounds like a good marriage to me!

I Made a Choice

As First Corinthians 15:21,22 says:

For since by man came death, by man came also the resurrection of the dead.

For as in Adam all die, even so in Christ shall all be made alive.

As we learned in the book of Genesis, the man was not deceived. He understood what was happening and he made a choice.

I had a choice in my life. I could have chosen to disobey God by staying in the corporate world. I could have chosen to have all the accolades that come with the money and the fame. I could have had all the admirations of men as a BUPPY — a black urban professional. People would have thought nicely of me, and no one would have said anything bad about me.

But I decided to obey God when He said to me: "Leave your job and go into the ministry. Take everything that you have and give it to Me, then do what I say. I am sending you to a place that you know not."

As it turned out, Oklahoma was "the place I knew not." It had happened to me as it did with Abraham when God told him to go to a certain place.

But people didn't understand it. Some said to me, "You aren't doing what's right for your wife." I was called a fool and told that I was stupid. My name got dragged through the mud. I had to endure a lot.

I lost all the praises of men. But I found out that when you lose the praise of men you gain the praise of God.

By obeying God, I received His anointing to carry out His Word. He anointed me when I preached, when I laid hands on the sick and when I cast out devils.

And guess what else happened? The derision of men was turned around. Those people stopped talking against me! Some of them even began to praise my actions.

Don't Blame God

So what happened after Adam and Eve chose to eat the fruit of that tree?

> **They heard the voice of the Lord God walking in the garden in the cool of the day: and Adam and his wife hid themselves from the presence of the Lord God amongst the trees of the garden.**
>
> **Genesis 3:8**

When Adam heard God's voice, he hid himself.

> **And the Lord God called unto Adam, and said unto him, Where art thou?**
>
> **Genesis 3:9**

God asked, "Where are you, Adam?" — as if He didn't know.

> **And he said, I heard thy voice in the garden, and I was afraid, because I was naked; and I hid myself.**
>
> **Genesis 3:10**

Adam was saying, "I hid myself, because I found out I was naked."

Both Adam and Eve lost that glory, that shine, which comes with walking in fellowship with God.

Then God asked Adam:

**Who told thee that thou wast naked? Hast thou
eaten of the tree, whereof I commanded thee that thou
shouldest not eat?**

Genesis 3:11

In other words, "Who told you that you were naked,
Adam? Did you eat the fruit of that tree I commanded you
not to eat?"

Then we see man doing what men are still doing today:

**And the man said, The woman whom thou gavest
to be with me, she gave me of the tree, and I did eat.**

Genesis 3:12

Something you will find out about Satan's nature is that
it always looks to establish blame somewhere else, saying,
"It's not *my* fault; it's somebody else's fault."

The first thing Adam started to do was to put the blame
on someone else. Instead of admitting to God, "Yes, I did
it," he wouldn't even acknowledge it. In fact, he blamed
God even before he blamed the woman. Notice how he
phrased his statement:

**The woman whom *thou* gavest to be with me, she
gave me of the tree.**

In other words, "*You* gave me this woman, God. I knew
the tree was there, but I didn't bother it. *She* bothered the
tree. *She's* the one who did it, and *You're* the One Who gave
her to me."

Are you always trying to blame God for your troubles?
If so, it's time you stopped blaming God for what has
happened in your life. It wasn't God's fault. Remember,
God isn't your problem; He's your answer.

The Blame Game

Immediately after blaming God, Adam then turned the
blame toward the woman, saying, "It was that woman —
she did it!"

So God asked her about it:

And the Lord God said unto the woman, What is this that thou hast done? And the woman said, The serpent beguiled me, and I did eat.

Genesis 3:13

When God asked her what she had done, then she started playing the blame game. She said, "It was that serpent. *He* beguiled me. *He* tricked me." But she didn't continue by confessing to God, "...and I listened to him." Like Adam, she refused to admit her mistake.

They both were acting contrary to God's way. Later, Jesus came to take our sins upon Himself. (1 Cor. 15:3; 1 John 4:10.) First John 1:9 says:

If we confess our sins, he is faithful and just to forgive us our sins, and to cleanse us from all unrighteousness.

Whenever you sin, you might be able to hide it from your pastor and other people, but you can never hide it from God. God always sees what is going on, so don't think you can get away with it. You need to repent of that sin and change your way of living.

As a believer, you are not to be living with a person out of wedlock. That's sin! Being involved in sexual intercourse with someone other than your mate will keep you in sin! Just remember: God is watching. So if that's your problem, you need to stop right now and repent of it!

Ladies, I don't care what your man may have told you. Maybe he has said: "Baby, I love you."

Let me tell you emphatically: There is no such thing as love without commitment. But there is plenty of lust without commitment. Lots of people are confusing lust with love, but they aren't the same. Love is entirely different from lust. Love requires commitment. So remember: no commitment — no love. The commitment God expects between a man and woman is lifelong. It's real commitment.

God Cursed the Serpent

God then turned to the serpent:

> **And the Lord God said unto the serpent, Because thou hast done this, thou art cursed above all cattle, and above every beast of the field; upon thy belly shalt thou go, and dust shalt thou eat all the days of thy life:**
>
> **And I will put enmity between thee and the woman, and between thy seed and her seed; it shall bruise thy head, and thou shalt bruise his heel.**
>
> **Genesis 3:14,15**

God didn't ask the serpent any questions as He had the man and the woman. Prior to this, the serpent had obviously walked upright, but God just spoke a curse to it, saying: "Because of this, you are to be cursed. You will crawl on your belly and eat dust for the rest of your life."

In verse 15 God talked about the enmity between the serpent and the woman, between her seed and his seed. Satan hates all of mankind, but he particularly hates women. He does everything he can to hurt women and has particularly targeted them through the centuries. Women have been abused throughout all of creation.

7

Husband and Wife

Therefore shall a man leave his father and his mother, and shall cleave unto his wife: and they shall be one flesh.

Genesis 2:24

Notice this Scripture does not say a *woman* shall leave her father and mother; it says *man*. If he is still at home with Mama and Daddy, he isn't a man yet, but hopefully he is working on it.

Man Must Assume Responsibility

A person becomes a man when he has gotten out from under Daddy and Mama's footsteps — when he has taken a job and is maturing in life. Until that happens, he is a male but not a man! There is a difference. All of us in the male species were born a male, but we could live and die without ever becoming a man. You see, God fashioned man with responsibility.

Our son is still at home. He is only eighteen years old, but he is growing into manhood by learning to accept responsibility. He is about to go to college, so that's work he is assuming. As long as he is willing to take on work, he can still have access to all the goodies of our home. But as he matures, he will have to reach the place where he gets a job and leaves his father and mother. This should be before a woman comes into his life.

From Mama to Wife

No woman should be joined to a man when he is coming right out of his mama's house. That means he hasn't yet learned how to be on his own. He is still under the care of his mama. She still fixes his meals, presses his clothes and makes his favorite dessert. He can leave his clothes lying around his room, but before he gets home, Mama will have put everything away.

One reason men don't learn to cook or to clean is because they never really leave home. They just go from Mama to wife. They should be going from Mama, to job, to being out on their own before they ever try to find a wife.

This is why there are still so many boys at home when they should become men who are out on their own. Only after moving out from under their parents' eyes will they really learn to operate responsibly. Then they will be able to do the work God gives them.

Man's Need for Self-Sufficiency

Men should not be marrying at such a young age like nineteen or twenty. For a woman to see some maturity in a man, she needs to wait until he gets a little older and has learned to become self-sufficient before she marries him.

For him to really be joined to his wife means he has to be separated from his mama and daddy.

Some people are out of the will of God because they allow their mamas and daddies to keep their noses in their children's business. Or they keep running back to Mama and Daddy every time something happens, saying, "My husband did this..." or "My wife did that...."

Neither mate should be running back and telling their parents about their marital problems. They should stay in there and get it worked out themselves with God's help. If necessary, they can go to the other provision God has made for them: the Church. For them to take their marital problems back to Mama and Daddy just makes things worse. That's not really their parents' business.

Let's say a husband and wife are having a problem. If she goes and tells Mama about what has happened, Mama gets upset and says, "I'll kill that jerk!" Then Mama tells everybody else in the family. When Daddy hears about it, he says, "I'm getting my shotgun!"

But two days later the husband comes home with flowers and a card. He gets down on his knees and apologizes to her, saying, "I'm sorry, baby. I was stupid. I shouldn't have done that. Will you forgive me, please?" So the wife accepts him back at once, and it's makeup time. Then both of them are smiling and happy.

But guess what? Her parents are still fuming. The husband and wife may forgive each other, but Mama and Daddy will never forgive!

Who's Pursuing Who?

God's order of things is the way to go. Again, Genesis 2:24 says:

> **Therefore shall a man leave his father and his mother, and shall cleave unto his wife: and they shall be one flesh.**

The word *cleave* in the Hebrew means "to pursue hard, be joined together, stick to."[1] That shouldn't be hard for the man to do. After taking one look at her, he wants to pursue hard after her.

The man is to be perpetually chasing after the woman, and she is to be doing all the things to cause him to be perpetually chasing her. When either of them stops doing what they are supposed to do, then their marriage can break down.

While he was chasing after her, she did lots of wonderful things to keep him interested. She dressed a certain way for him and always wore some new perfume. She kept teasing him, and he just kept coming back for more.

She smiled when he walked through the door. She may have been sitting there talking with somebody else, but when she saw him, she smiled at him and then he saw her. He thought she was the cheeriest, most wonderful person he had ever seen.

She never let him see her without makeup. If by accident he did, she would say, "Wait a minute. I can look better!" She would leave the room and not come back until she had everything combed and fixed and straightened. She was always looking and acting so nice. (And he was supposed to be the one pursuing her!)

I remember when I pursued Deborah. I was always calling her, but she wouldn't say very much. When I asked her why she wasn't talking, she said, "I just like hearing your voice." That was all I needed to hear! Then I just wanted to take her places and buy her things. I would say, "Where do you want to go? What can I get for you?" I didn't watch much TV; I was at her house all the time. I just wanted to be with her.

In the dating process, the woman lets the man chase her until she gets him! Then after marriage, her ideas change. She thinks, *I have him now, so I don't care what he likes. I'm dressing for me!* In fact, after marriage, things change for both of them. She won't sit next to him anymore, and he forgets her birthday. When either of them break their roles, trouble sets in.

One Flesh

Let's look at this Scripture again:

> **Therefore shall a man leave his father and his mother, and shall cleave unto his wife: and they shall be one flesh.**
>
> **Genesis 2:24**

Note the last phrase of this verse: ...**and they shall be one flesh.** It's important for you to realize that sex isn't dirty; it was God's idea. God created it, and anything God created is good. But men have made it dirty.

Over the years people have said to me: "Pastor, we don't need to get married. All we have to do is come together like in the Bible. We don't need some piece of paper to tell us we're married."

But that kind of thinking is wrong. Law says it takes that piece of paper to verify the marriage. In Romans, chapter 13, God's Word says we are, first of all, to respect the laws of the land. (v. 1.)

I have heard people use Adam and Eve as their excuse, saying, "But *they* didn't have a wedding ceremony."

My question then is, Who would have come to their ceremony anyway? Just animals, I guess. (And there was no bridal shower for her, either.) But there still was a marriage. God was the One Who brought the woman to the man, and God joined them together in marriage.

In fact, chapter 3, verse 8, says:

And they heard the voice of the Lord God walking in the garden in the cool of the day: and *Adam and his wife* hid themselves....

So the woman had become Adam's wife. God had performed the first marriage ceremony, telling the man to cleave unto his wife.

Sometimes a man might be having a fight with his wife, or a woman might be having a fight with her husband.

The wife may say to him, "You aren't my daddy!" That's right. He isn't her daddy; he is more than her daddy — far more. He has much more authority over her than her daddy does.

The husband may say to his wife, "You're not my mama!" No, she isn't; she is more than his mama. She has more than enough right to tell him about things that are happening in their lives.

As Genesis 2:24 says, the man is supposed to leave father and mother. It does not say he is to *leave* his wife; it says he is to *cleave* unto his wife.

Marriage: A Threefold Covenant

I want us to look now in the book of Malachi. I might be sticking my nose into your business, but did you know it's the pastor's job to meddle in other people's business? That's what shepherds do: they get right in the middle of their sheep.

As chapter 2 of Genesis tells us, the wife was created as a helpmeet for the man, to be his capable spouse and to fit herself to him.

We see here that the children of Israel got themselves into trouble for messing around with this very subject:

> **And this have ye done again, covering the altar of the Lord with tears, with weeping, and with crying out, insomuch that he regardeth not the offering any more, or receiveth it with good will at your hand.**
>
> **Malachi 2:13**

These men wanted God to receive their sacrifice and to bless the works of their hands, but He would not receive it. They cried and bawled and wailed at the altar, but God still would not receive it.

> **Yet ye say, Wherefore?** [or, "Why, God?"] **Because the Lord hath been witness between thee and the wife of thy youth, against whom thou hast dealt treacherously: yet is she thy companion, and the wife of thy covenant.**
>
> **Malachi 2:14**

When joining in marriage, a man and woman are not just entering into a contract with the state; they are entering into a threefold covenant. There are three beings involved in this covenant: the husband, the wife and Almighty God. When entering into marriage, the husband and wife are making a covenant with God. How God deals with them will be based upon how they deal with their covenant.

These men of Israel were not dealing rightly with the wives of their youth. They had married young, but after getting older and becoming wealthy and established, they were shedding their wives for a younger model.

The Lord was saying to them: "I am not receiving anything from you. I am not blessing your hand or doing anything for you, because you have dealt treacherously with the wife of your youth. She is your covenant partner. She was there when you had nothing, and she should be receiving the fruit of that which you now have."

My wife is supposed to receive the benefits now accrued her, because she was with me when I had nothing. Because I have been blessed, Deborah ought to share in those blessings. Just because she is reaching forty does not mean I can turn her in for a twenty-year-old. This is what those men were doing in the book of Malachi.

Let's keep reading here in verse 15:

And did not he [God] make one?...

In other words, "Did not God make the husband and wife to be as one?"

In Genesis 2:24 we read how God made the man and the woman one — one in name, aim, purpose, thought and direction.

And did not he [God] make one? Yet had he the residue of the spirit. And wherefore one? That he might seek a godly seed....

Malachi 2:15

God wants a godly seed. He wants a born-again man and a born-again woman to have children. Now I'm talking here in general; I'm not referring to individual cases. There are some married couples who, for various reasons, should not have children. But, as a whole, God is seeking a godly seed.

God Hates Divorce

...Therefore take heed to your spirit, and let none deal treacherously against the wife of his youth.

For the Lord, the God of Israel, saith that *he hateth putting away*: for one covereth violence with his garment, saith the Lord of hosts: therefore take heed to your spirit, that ye deal not treacherously.

Malachi 2:15,16

What is this Scripture saying in verse 16? That God **hateth putting away**, referring to divorce.

Notice how verse 16 reads from *The Amplified Bible:*

For the Lord, the God of Israel, says: I hate divorce and marital separation, and him who covers his garment [his wife] with violence. Therefore keep a watch upon your spirit [that it may be controlled by My Spirit], that you deal not treacherously and faithlessly [with your marriage mate].

God hates divorce, but He still loves those who happen to be involved in divorce.

Divorce was not in God's original plan. God had intended for the man to stick to and cling to his wife all the days of their lives. He had intended for the woman to be a help to her husband, but not to run his life. Together they would be doing what God had intended for them to do.

Jesus' Attitude Toward Marriage

Then in Matthew, chapter 19, we read what Jesus said about this subject of divorce:

The Pharisees also came unto him, tempting him, and saying unto him, Is it lawful for a man to put away his wife for every cause?

> **And he answered and said unto them, Have ye not read, that he which made them at the beginning made them male and female,**
>
> **And said, For this cause shall a man leave father and mother, and shall cleave to his wife: and they twain shall be one flesh?**
>
> **Wherefore they are no more twain, but one flesh. What therefore God hath joined together [which means marriage], let not man put asunder.**
>
> **Matthew 19:3-6**

Male and Female From the Beginning

Notice verse 4:

> **And he answered and said unto them, Have ye not read, that he which made them at the beginning made them male and female.**
>
> **Matthew 19:4**

Jesus was saying that from the beginning God made them both male and female. He did not make them to be male and male or female and female.

Some people have the idea that homosexuals were born that way. But that's not true; they weren't born that way. Now maybe things happened to them when they were too young to recollect which caused a change in their lives, but they weren't born that way.

God made male, and He made female. That's the only way we are to be when joining ourselves together in marriage.

They Shall Be One Flesh

Then Jesus, quoting from the book of Genesis, says:

> **For this cause shall a man leave father and mother, and shall cleave to his wife: and they twain shall be one flesh.**
>
> **Matthew 19:5**

Now the wife cannot be telling her husband, "You need to give me some space." He is to cleave to her, and she should be glad of that. His instinct is to keep her close and stick to her; so when he sees her, he wants to touch her.

But then she says, "I can't seem to wear a certain kind of clothes. When I do, my husband won't leave me alone!"

Does that mean she would want him to be messing with some other woman? I doubt it.

> **...and they twain shall be one flesh?**
> **Wherefore they are no more twain, but one flesh.**
> **What therefore God hath joined together** [meaning marriage], **let not man put asunder.**
> **Matthew 19:5,6**

Remember Jesus' words: **What therefore God hath joined together....** Now it may not have been the will of God for one person to have married another, but when they made their vows and said, "I do," it became the will of God.

God Never Wanted Divorce

> **They say unto him, Why did Moses then command to give a writing of divorcement, and to put her away?**
> **He saith unto them, Moses because of the hardness of your hearts suffered you to put away your wives: but from the beginning** [meaning in Genesis] **it was not so.**
> **Matthew 19:7,8**

In the beginning, God never intended for there to be divorce. He intended for a man to always be with his wife — and that was it. But God allowed man to go through stages and do what he wanted to do. Man did what was good in his own sight; and as described in the book of Malachi, he dealt treacherously.

We could look back through the book of Genesis and see what happened when men had their own way. They messed up, allowing sin to run their lives, and destruction came as a result.

The Law was established as a way to point out man's failure and to show him that he needed a Deliverer — and deliverance. Men were putting away their wives for no reason at all.

In Old Covenant days, a husband could give a writ of divorcement for any cause. If he wasn't satisfied with his wife's cooking, he could divorce her. But that was never the will of God.

Today we can see this happening again. The wife or husband can be put away for any cause. It's called no-fault divorce. But there really is no such thing.

"It Is Not Good to Marry"

Jesus said:

> **And I say unto you, Whosoever shall put away his wife, except it be for fornication, and shall marry another, committeth adultery: and whoso marrieth her which is put away doth commit adultery.**
>
> **His disciples say unto him, If the case of the man be so with his wife, it is not good to marry.**
>
> **Matthew 19:9,10**

The disciples were saying, "If we can't get rid of a woman whenever we want to, then we shouldn't get married." Do you see their attitude?

While at the University of Michigan, I attended a class on marriage and family. I remember the professor standing up and saying to all the men in that class, "If you marry a woman, you're a fool. A man should never *marry* a woman; he should just live with her."

The foolish women in that class were swallowing everything the professor said. But just because the professor at a university says it still doesn't make it so.

I put up my hand and asked if I could speak. Then I gave an objection to his statement. As a result, he marked my grade down. I had to make an official appeal over it; but I won.

Jesus' Words About Eunuchs

The disciples were saying, "It's not good to marry."

Jesus responded by saying to them:

> **All men cannot receive this saying** [of being without a wife], **save they to whom it is given.**
>
> **For there are some eunuchs, which were so born from their mother's womb....**
>
> Matthew 19:11,12

Jesus was saying that certain ones were born that way — but not as homosexuals, as eunuchs.

> **...and there are some eunuchs, which were made eunuchs of men....**
>
> Matthew 19:12

In other words, Jesus was telling how some men have declared to others, "In order for you to operate with us, this is how you must be." We find this happening, for example, with Catholic priests who take an oath of celebacy.

> **...and there be eunuchs, which have made themselves eunuchs for the kingdom of heaven's sake....**
>
> Matthew 19:12

Such people have made this decision because they desire to serve the Lord with all their time and energy. That's all they want to do.

> **...He that is able to receive it, let him receive it.**
>
> Matthew 19:12

Jesus was telling us that some men aren't capable of being celibate. In this case, He was saying to them, "Then you should get a wife."

Husband and Wife Are as One

I want to show you something else about Genesis 2:24: **Therefore shall a man leave his father and his mother, and shall cleave unto his wife: and they shall be one flesh.** Again, the husband and wife are to be as one flesh, clinging hard to one another. She is to help him and adapt herself to him.

Let's look at Genesis, chapter 5:

> **This is the book of the generations of Adam. In the day that God created man** [day six in the Creation], **in the likeness of God made he him;**
>
> **Male and female created he them; and blessed them, and called** *their* **name Adam, in the day when they were created.**
>
> **Genesis 5:1,2**

When *they* were first created, it was not as Adam and Eve. *They* were Adam — a male Adam and a female Adam. God fashioned this woman and built her from the man. Then He brought her unto Adam. God called the male, *Adam*, and He called the female, *Adam*. It was Adam who gave her a name. He looked at her and said, **she shall be called Woman, because she was taken out of Man** (Gen. 2:23). God was saying, "They are as one, so they will have the same name."

The practice of a woman taking upon herself her husband's name comes from the Bible. When a woman marries a man, she takes his name as she becomes his helpmeet. As his helpmeet, she is to fold herself into him, and they become one.

Today the world is teaching that the woman should keep her own name and identity.

For a woman to say she isn't going to take her husband's name is a statement of defiance to God; it is a defiance of her role against his. To do this is for her to be asking for trouble right from the start.

There is a basic attitude involved between the husband and wife in marriage. They each have a role. But God sees the husband and wife as one the way He saw Adam and Eve as one. Again, the Scripture says He **called** *their* **name Adam**.

My wife's name is no longer Deborah Bell, but Deborah Butler. When she married me, we became one in name, aim, purpose, thought and direction. It was a call from God.

All of that individualistic thinking left. She is in me, and I am in her. Where I end, she begins; and where she ends, I begin. What God has joined together let not man put asunder with humanistic ideas — be they from man or from woman. God knows best.

Husband To Love the Wife as Christ Loves the Church

The New Testament clearly establishes man as the head of the home, but he is to rule his home with all the love that is in him. Let's look at Ephesians 5:25. It says:

Husbands, love your wives, even as Christ also loved the church, and gave himself for it.

The husband is to treat his wife as Christ treats the Church, and Christ loves the Church. The Lord is so patient and kind and loving toward us. Even when we mess up, He still loves us. God is so good to His children. The husband is to be the same way toward his wife.

Endnote

[1]Strong, "Hebrew," p. 29, #1692.

8
Punishment for Disobedience

We know that after Adam sinned, both of them — male Adam and female Adam — died spiritually. As a result, certain punishments came with the Fall which greatly affected the way they would live their lives. We will read about this from Genesis, chapter 3.

Woman's Punishment in Childbirth

Unto the woman he said, I will greatly multiply thy sorrow and thy conception; in sorrow thou shalt bring forth children; and thy desire shall be to thy husband, and he shall rule over thee.

Genesis 3:16

The woman had originally been created to bring forth children. In the beginning God told them to be fruitful and to multiply. He always intended for the woman to bear children, or else they could not possibly have multiplied as God had expected them to do at that time.

But God had not originally intended for woman to suffer the pains of childbirth and all the problems that come with pregnancy, such as morning sickness. The birth of human babies could have been like that of the animals. Generally, the birth of animals is not a difficult experience for the mothers; those tiny creatures are born in a matter-of-fact sort of way. But part of woman's punishment for disobeying God was having to face sorrow in childbirth.

Her Husband To Rule Over Her

Looking again at Genesis 3:16, note another aspect of the woman's punishment:

> **Unto the woman he said, I will greatly multiply thy sorrow and thy conception; in sorrow thou shalt bring forth children; *and thy desire shall be to thy husband,* and he shall rule over thee.**

The Hebrew word for "desire" means "stretching out after, a longing, desire."[1]

The woman's desire will be stretched out always for her husband. In other words, she has a strong desire for him. She longs for him. She can't do without him.

> **...and thy desire shall be to thy husband, and he shall rule over thee.**

The word for "rule" means "to have power over."[2] In other words, this verse was saying, "He shall have power over thee."

Apparently God originally intended for man and woman to operate a little differently from this, but things changed after they chose to disobey God's commandment.

Promise of Redemption for the Woman's Punishment

In the New Testament, the redeemed woman is born again through the blood of Jesus Christ. As a result, she has been given hope in this situation. Let's look in First Timothy, chapter 2:

> **For Adam was first formed, then Eve.**
>
> **And Adam was not deceived, but the woman being deceived was in the transgression.**
>
> **Notwithstanding she shall be saved in childbearing, *if* they continue in faith and charity [love] and holiness with sobriety.**
>
> **1 Timothy 2:13-15**

This Scripture says the woman **shall be saved in childbearing** *if* she takes on the lifestyle of a true believer. She must be a woman of faith, a woman who operates in God's love and a woman who lives seriously before God.

She can believe God that her pregnancy will not be nine months of morning sickness or other problems, followed by intense, overwhelming labor pains at the time of birth.

Now my wife and I have three children. At the birth of our first child we were saved, but we had not learned this truth from God's Word. As a result, Deborah suffered in intense labor for seventeen hours.

That was the first time I had ever been in a maternity ward. I was only twenty years old at the time, and it was something to behold. Deborah was in a private room, but next to her was a ward full of pregnant women. All of them were about to deliver their babies, and they were screaming and hollering. Some were cursing their husbands and even cursing God.

Our first experience with pregnancy was a tough one. But before the second pregnancy, we found this Scripture in First Timothy that says, **...if they continue in faith....**

After learning this New Testament promise, we began to believe God. As a result, Deborah did not have the same kind of experience with our two baby girls that she had with the first pregnancy. In fact, her labor with each of the girls took no more than two hours.

Man's Punishment

Then God spoke to Adam after he had disobeyed:

> **And unto Adam he said, Because thou hast hearkened unto the voice of thy wife** [or, "Because you chose her over Me"], **and hast eaten of the tree, of which I commanded thee, saying, Thou shalt not eat of it: cursed is the ground for thy sake; in sorrow shalt thou eat of it all the days of thy life.**
>
> **Genesis 3:17**

Remember, God gave Adam a job to do before He gave him the woman. But the job Adam had to do was easy. God had given him dominion over everything. If he had spoken to the ground, it would have yielded to him.

It was after Adam had disobeyed that God told him how hard things were going to be. God said, **Cursed is the ground for thy sake; in sorrow shalt thou eat of it all the days of thy life.** God was describing to him how difficult the work would be all the days of his life.

God did not create man so that he could sit down and do nothing after reaching retirement age. Now I'm not saying that man has to be doing strenuous work every day of his life, but God never intended for him to go and sit by the ocean for the rest of his days.

Notice the words from God to Adam in verses 18 and 19:

> **Thorns also and thistles shall it bring forth to thee; and thou shalt eat the herb of the field;**
> **In the sweat of thy face shalt thou eat bread, till thou return unto the ground** [or until you die]**; for out of it wast thou taken: for dust thou art, and unto dust shalt thou return.**

God was saying to the man, "Your punishment is that you will have to do hard labor all the days of your life." God's punishment to man called for him to have sweat on his face all of his life. Notice that this punishment was given to the man, not the woman.

Now I am not saying that it's a sin for a woman to work. But she wasn't made to do work as hard as a man. That wasn't her punishment; it was his. She is different from him. She wasn't made to spend hours and hours slaving at a job. If she chooses to do it and he chooses to send her out, that's a different matter. But she wasn't made to do it.

Neither should the husband be complaining to his wife about how she just sits around the house while he is out there working. The wife isn't supposed to be working like him.

The wife has been given a different kind of job: to take care of her husband. Her desire should be for him. When he comes home with sweat on his brow, it's her responsibility to take care of him. She should make sure she has the time so that she can care for him in the right way.

God really intended for man to do the sweating. He intended for woman to be involved in taking care of her man and keeping their home, which is quite a job. In fact, it's a higher job for her to do than working for some big company.

But today's liberal world has reached a place where it is demeaning toward woman's important role of raising a godly seed. As a result, women have started working in many of the same jobs as men, and their bodies are breaking down quicker because of it. They weren't made to operate that way.

Man's Punishment Modified, But Not Removed

As we have learned, man's punishment in the Garden of Eden was to work hard all the days of his life. But when he gets born again by making Jesus Christ the Lord of his life, man's punishment can be modified, as is childbearing for the woman.

As it should be, the intensity of punishment will be reduced from that which we initially found in Genesis when man had sinned and experienced spiritual death.

Man enters into a new way of life through faith in Christ Jesus. We step into the place where God intends for us to be: in His will for us according to His Word. Then work for us today isn't nearly as hard as it would be if we were living outside of God's will.

But man's punishments have not been completely removed, because we are still in this physical body. A new body is the last thing we will be getting.

Right now heaven and earth are travailing, waiting for that day when the Lord comes and re-creates the earth again. Then there will be a new heaven and a new earth. The closer we get to the time of the end, there will be more travailing as we experience earthquakes and other natural disasters.

But There Is Still Work To Do

It's good to know that the reborn man of the New Testament is not bound by the punishment we found in Genesis. But don't get me wrong: he still has to work. He can't just sit down and say, 'I'm a believer, so I don't have to work now. I'll just believe I receive! So bless me, Father!" That's not what I'm saying!

God has given us a job to do, but that job is just one of many tools which the Lord has provided for us. We are to walk by faith as we work to give and bless those who are in need.

Providing for Others

Once again, let me say that no believer can just quit working because he has decided to "live by faith." First Timothy 5:8 is a strong statement of judgment toward such a believer. It says:

But if any provide not for his own, and specially for those of his own house, he hath denied the faith, and is worse than an infidel.

Obviously, there is a difference between "his own" and "his own house." The Greek word translated *house* in this verse means his kindred, his blood.[3]

In other words, a man is not to be providing just for his own children, but he is to be a blessing to others. We are not to be selfish.

This can be a problem between husbands and wives. Suppose the husband wants to give some money to bless his brother who is in trouble, but the wife disagrees. Or maybe the wife sees that she and her husband have the means to be a blessing to her sister who has needs, but the husband disagrees. The result is, they fight over it. They could even split up because of it.

Every believer should be willing to bless others when he is capable of doing so.

Denying the Faith
and Worse Than an Infidel

Again, First Timothy 5:8 says:

> **If any provide not for his own, and specially for those of his own house, he hath denied the faith, and is worse than an infidel.**

By denying the faith, this person wants nothing to do with it and has turned his back on it. As this Scripture says he is worse than an infidel, or an unbeliever. An unbeliever is going to hell, but the person who denies the faith is even worse than that.

Be a Word Man!

So God intends for the New Testament believer to work and to be a blessing to others. He is to live by faith and become a Word man. He must know and act on Scriptures like Luke 6:38, which says:

> **Give, and it shall be given unto you; good measure, pressed down, and shaken together, and running over....**

The husband who doesn't pray and spend time in the Word will never be living like that. Instead, he will be like the Genesis man, who knows only sweat in his brow. There will be no faith at work in his life. He will always have a bad attitude and be angry, feeling that he isn't appreciated.

The most spiritual person in the home is supposed to be the husband, but too often it's the wife. He should be the one who says to her, "I believe God is telling me that we are to bless that individual, so let's do it."

The wife's desire should be to support her husband. When he says that, she should respond by saying, "Honey, you're the leader. I believe you are hearing from God, so let's go be a blessing."

Man To Provide for His Own

As God's Word says, a man is to provide for his own: **...specially for those of his own house...** (1 Tim. 5:8). That's why the issue has developed about men who have fathered children but refuse to pay child support. A man is to provide for his own, especially for those of his own house; in other words, his own kids.

If, God forbid, a woman is separated from the father of her children, that man has the legal responsibility to take care of those kids. But even more than that, he has a biblical responsibility as their father.

If the husband leaves and isn't taking care of his children, something should be done about it.

The wife should never back away, saying things like: "But I don't want to make him upset or to hurt him." If necessary, she should go to court and see about having his wages attached. Then provision will be made for their kids.

In this situation, however, we need to realize that money for child support does not belong to the mother. The purpose of that money is to provide for the children's needs, not so that the mother can use it to buy herself a new dress.

This brings us to the other side of the coin.

Sometimes it's hard to blame the men. The father sends money for his kids, but the mother takes advantage of it and spends that money on herself. That's wrong. In effect, she is stealing, and there should be a law against it. If the father has to go to jail for not providing child support, the mother should also have to pay the price for stealing from those kids and using it on herself.

In either case, the children deserve the support of both mother and father.

A man who won't take care of his children isn't a man; he's just a male. The instinct in a male dog is to father pups and then move on. The true instinct in a man should be to care for and provide for his own. That's what God intended.

Woman Was Named Eve

In the Old Testament, we have seen God's punishments that were set against both man and woman, but in the New Testament, we have seen some provisions for them.

Remember in Genesis, chapter 1, we learned that God gave the planet to Adam — the male and the female. He was saying to them, "You have dominion, or rulership, over every living thing upon the earth. You are to rule this planet."

But when the man and the woman sinned, they bowed their knees to Satan. The woman was tricked, but the man was not. He was unwilling to stand and take his rightful place of authority and dominion over this earth.

What happened then? Satan became the god of this world. (2 Cor. 4:4.) The rulership over this world, which God had given to man, was passed to the devil, and his satanic nature showed up immediately. When the man and woman sinned, they died spiritually, and Satan gained spiritual authority in the earth.

It was only after they received their punishment that Adam gave woman the name, Eve. As the Scripture says:

> **And Adam called his wife's name Eve; because she was the mother of all living.**
>
> **Genesis 3:20**

Endnote

[1]Strong, "Hebrew," p. 126, #8669.

[2]Ibid., p. 74, #4910.

[3]*The Holy Bible, King James Version.* (Camden, NJ: Thomas Nelson, 1972), p. 255, footnote #3, First Timothy 5:8.

9

The Sexual Union

And Adam knew Eve his wife; and she conceived, and bare Cain, and said, I have gotten a man from the Lord.

Genesis 4:1

The first few words in this verse tell us part of God's plan:

And Adam *knew* Eve his wife....

When the Bible says Adam *knew* her, it doesn't mean he just knew who she was or knew her address. It means he knew her as his wife. In other words, he had sexual relations with her.

God is the Author of sex. He created it and developed it. Sex was God's idea, not man's. In and of itself, sex isn't dirty and it isn't perverted; but it can be. There have been some dirty things made out of it, and there are limits to its use.

A Husband Is To Be With *His* Wife

Notice this Scripture says, **And Adam knew Eve *his* wife....** *His* wife is the only one Adam was supposed to know sexually.

God's plan has a certain order to it: He wants each man to be joined sexually with his own wife, and no other person. An unmarried man should not know *any* woman sexually until after he has exchanged marriage vows with her.

Notice that Eve gave proper credit to God as the Source of her first child. The Scripture says:

> **And Adam knew Eve his wife; and she conceived, and bare Cain, and said,** *I have gotten a man from the Lord.*

> **Genesis 4:1**

Once again, God is the One Who gives life. Man and woman physically come together in the sexual union, but it is God Who puts life into their child. Therefore, only God has the right to take that life.

Even in the New Testament, we have laid out for us what God's plan is for mankind, how He intended for everything to operate in a certain order. God has an order for everything, with everything being in its proper place.

Sex Is Not a Weapon!

I want us to look at some verses in First Corinthians, chapter 7:

> **Now concerning the things whereof ye wrote unto me: It is good for a man not to touch a woman.**

> **Nevertheless, to avoid fornication, let every man have his own wife, and let every woman have her own husband.**

> **Let the husband render unto the wife due benevolence: and likewise also the wife unto the husband.**

> **The wife hath not power of her own body, but the husband: and likewise also the husband hath not power of his own body, but the wife.**

> **Defraud ye not one the other, except it be with consent for a time, that ye may give yourselves to fasting and prayer; and come together again, that Satan tempt you not for your incontinency [or lack of self-control].**

> **1 Corinthians 7:1-5**

Now I want us to look at this passage of Scripture from *The Amplified Bible*, beginning with verse 2:

> **But because of the temptation to impurity and to avoid immorality, let each [man] have his own wife and let each [woman] have her own husband.**
>
> **The husband should give to his wife her conjugal rights** [meaning the right to have sex with her husband] **— goodwill, kindness and what is due her as his wife; and likewise the wife to her husband.**
>
> **For the wife does not have [exclusive] authority and control over her own body, but the husband [has his rights]; likewise also the husband does not have [exclusive] authority and control over his body, but the wife [has her rights].**
>
> **Do not refuse and deprive and defraud each other (of your due marital rights), except perhaps by mutual consent for a time, that you may devote yourselves unhindered to prayer. But afterwards resume marital relations, lest Satan tempt you [to sin] through your lack of restraint of sexual desire.**

Now it was, and always has been, God's plan that a man and woman be married. Then, as now, they are to *have one another* as husband and wife. Note verse 2 from the *King James Version*:

> **Let every man *have* his own wife, and let every woman *have* her own husband.**

God intended for a man to *have* only his wife and for a woman to *have* only her husband — period.

It was never God's plan for man and woman to use sex as a weapon against each other. Regardless of whether or not you are saved, for you to use sex as a weapon by withholding it from your spouse is to be out of God's plan, out of God's will, out of God's Word. That means it's wrong!

Sex Involves More Than Procreation

God intended for a husband and his wife to join themselves together physically, but not just for procreation purposes.

Remember, in the Old Testament God told the man and woman to be fruitful *and* multiply. (Gen. 1:28.) But in First Corinthians, chapter 7, the apostle Paul in talking about the marriage union did not mention anything about procreation or about the couple's need to have children. He was clearly describing the significance of sexual relations between a husband and wife.

Now this is important, because people can get themselves into trouble. Either the husband or the wife could end up getting involved in an extramarital affair if their spouse has refused to fulfil their sexual needs.

The Obligation of Sex Between Husband and Wife

Note what it says in verse 4 of First Corinthians, chapter 7:

> **The wife hath not power of her own body, but the husband: and likewise also the husband hath not power of his own body, but the wife.**

Recently an article in the newspaper talked about how sex can help to cure the headache and that it is healthy for the body. I happen to believe that, not because I'm a man, but because I have studied the Bible. Anything designed by God is good.

> **The wife hath not power of her own body, but the husband...** (v. 4).

This means the wife has an obligation to involve herself sexually with her husband when he desires it.

Verse 4 continues by saying:

> **...and likewise also the husband hath not power of his own body, but the wife.**

This means the husband should not come dragging in and say to his wife, "I'm tired; leave me alone." He has the obligation to perform sexually for her, just as he would expect her to give herself sexually to him. That's God's intention. It's the will of God, and people get into trouble when they step out of God's will.

As verse 5 says:

Defraud ye not one the other, except it be with consent for a time, that ye may give yourselves to fasting and prayer....

So there are times of fasting and prayer when the husband and wife should not involve themselves with sexual relations. But after that time, it says they are to **...come together again, that Satan tempt you not for your incontinency** [or lack of self-control].

So God intended for man and woman to experience sex, but only after marriage. Within the marital union, God intended for sex to be not just for the procreation of children but as a way to enjoy each other. That is God's plan for man.

When things are done in proper order the way God has set them up, then blessings will come.

Now we are talking about God's plan for man that was from the very beginning when, as Scripture says, **Adam** *knew* **Eve his wife.** God intended for that to be.

No Sex Outside Marriage!

Let's look now in First Corinthians, chapter 6:

Know ye not that the unrighteous shall not inherit the kingdom of God? Be not deceived: neither fornicators, nor idolaters, nor adulterers [that's extramarital sex], **nor effeminate** [referring to homosexuality], **nor abusers of themselves with mankind,**

Nor thieves, nor covetous, nor drunkards, nor revilers, nor extortioners, shall inherit the kingdom of God.

Verses 9,10

95

Fornication is sex outside the legal marriage union. Clearly, God frowns on premarital or extramarital sex, both of which occur outside marriage.

God is saying, "Those who practice a lifestyle of such things shall not inherit the kingdom of God." This lifestyle puts such people outside of God's plan. In fact, verse 13 of this chapter says:

> **Meats for the belly, and the belly for meats: but God shall destroy both it and them. Now the body is not for fornication, but for the Lord; and the Lord for the body.**

According to Scripture, any unmarried person must refrain from having sexual intercourse. God intended it to be between two married people who have committed their lives to each other.

Commitment Is Required

Real love always carries with it commitment. The sexual experience that occurs between two people without commitment is not love but lust, and lust is only a temporary thing.

God's plan is for man and woman to be committed to one another through marriage before they engage in sex. Herein lies the problem with today's society. So many people are living outside of God's plan. All they desire is sex without commitment, but much trouble will come as a result.

One of society's big problems today is illegitimacy. An illegitimate birth doesn't make the child bad, but it puts that child and its mother in an unfavorable situation.

Besides illegitimacy, there is the problem of folks being sexually involved with so many different people. As a result they open themselves up to all kinds of diseases, some of which could be disastrous to their life and health.

God is against sin because He knows sin will kill people. There is a price to be paid for living in sin. It harms anyone who has stepped outside of God's will. God loves the sinner but He hates the sin. He wants His people to be blessed by turning from their wicked ways and seeking His will for their lives. (2 Chron. 7:14.)

Let's read more from First Corinthians, chapter 6:

But he that is joined unto the Lord is one spirit (v. 17).

Whether married or single, every believer should be joined unto the Lord.

Flee Fornication!

Flee fornication. Every sin that a man doeth is without the body; but he that committeth fornication sinneth against his own body (v. 18).

Flee fornication. The word *flee* means to run away from.

It's interesting to me that the Scripture would use this kind of verbiage. When God's Word says we are to *flee* fornication, we are being told just how powerful the sex drive is. God created this drive as a healthy act performed between husband and wife. It was never intended as some special occurrence that comes about only once a year. But we can't be fooling around with it, either.

If you happen to be with someone who causes your liver to quiver, don't just say, "Oh, I can handle this." No, the Bible says you are to flee from fornication. That means to run from it! You need to get out of any situation that could lead you off into other problems.

Anytime you go outside the will of God and get over into Satan's domain where sin is, you are putting yourself at risk.

Glorify God With Your Body

What? know ye not that your body is the temple of the Holy Ghost which is in you, which ye have of God, and ye are not your own?

**For ye are bought with a price: therefore glorify
God in your body, and in your spirit, which are God's.**
1 Corinthians 6:19,20

God was saying to believers: "If you are not married,
glorify Me by constantly joining yourself to Me. Never join
yourself sexually to someone unless you are married to that
person."

If you are having difficulty in this area, remember First
Corinthians 7:2, which says, **Let every man have his own
wife, and let every woman have her own husband.** No
man or woman is to be involved in fornication.

Any woman dating a guy who wants to have sex
without marriage needs to either get rid of him or tell him,
"Sorry, honey. If you want me, let me see that wedding
ring."

There is no reason why a man would want to marry a
woman when she allows him to enjoy the fruits of marriage
without having to commit himself legally or spiritually.
There would be no incentive for him to marry her.

Now he may pretend that he will marry her, but why
should he? Things are going just fine for him. He is getting
all that he wants from her now without marriage. She is
taking care of him, fussing over him and cooking his meals.
Whenever he wants to go to bed, she's there for him. Until
he gets saved, he will have zero incentive to marry her. So
it's time for her to wise up.

10
God's Principle of Tithing

Now let's continue in Genesis, chapter 4:

> And Adam knew Eve his wife; and she conceived, and bare Cain, and said, I have gotten a man from the Lord.

> And she again bare his brother Abel. And Abel was a keeper of sheep, but Cain was a tiller of the ground.

> And in process of time it came to pass, that Cain brought of the fruit of the ground an offering unto the Lord.

> And Abel, he also brought of the firstlings of his flock and of the fat thereof. And the Lord had respect unto Abel and to his offering:

> But unto Cain and to his offering he had not respect. And Cain was very wroth, and his countenance fell.

> And the Lord said unto Cain, Why art thou wroth? and why is thy countenance fallen?

> If thou doest well, shalt thou not be accepted? and if thou doest not well, sin lieth at the door. And unto thee shall be his desire, and thou shalt rule over him.

> And Cain talked with Abel his brother: and it came to pass, when they were in the field, that Cain rose up against Abel his brother, and slew him.

Genesis 4:1-8

Here we see that Cain and Abel worked two different jobs. Abel tended sheep while Cain tilled the ground.

Now remember, when Adam and Eve sinned, they died spiritually. Spiritual death has a twofold definition: first,

99

being separated from God; and secondly, receiving Satan's nature. That satanic nature showed up right away in their children with their oldest son, Cain, killing his brother, Abel.

I want you to notice what happened to start this whole incident. Obviously after a process of time, they came to understand their need to offer a sacrifice unto God. God required it. So Cain brought the fruit of the ground as an offering to the Lord, while Abel brought what he had: the firstborn of the flock and the fat from it.

Abel and Cain

When Adam and his wife discovered they were naked, **they sewed fig leaves together, and made themselves aprons** (Gen. 3:7). This was not accepted by God, Who shed the innocent blood of animals to clothe them. (Gen. 3:21.)

This is the first instance where the shedding of blood was used to *cover* sin, allowing God to deal with Adam and his wife. Evidently, they taught this principle to their sons. Abel complied with his parents' instructions, but Cain did not. Cain's offering was principally rejected because it was not a *blood* sacrifice.

The Difference in the Offerings

What was the difference between these two offerings?

Abel brought unto God the first of all that he had received from the flock he was tending. But not only did he bring God the firstfruit, he brought Him the fat thereof. The word translated *fat* here means "the richest or choice part."[1] So Abel brought as an offering to God the first and the best that he had. It was a *blood* sacrifice.

The offering Cain brought to God was of the fruit of the ground, but his offering wasn't the first and it wasn't the richest part.

The First Act of Faith

Abel's act was the first act of faith recorded in the Scripture. Abel gave God the first that he had, and on top of that, it was the richest part; and he did it by faith.

In Paul's epistle to the Hebrews, chapter 11, we read about the faith acts by God's people. This chapter of Hebrews is commonly called the "faith hall of fame." That's where we find stories about Abraham and Noah and Moses and many other of the patriarchs.

But note that Abel was the first person referred to in this faith chapter:

> **By faith Abel offered unto God a more excellent sacrifice than Cain, by which he obtained witness that he was righteous, God testifying of his gifts: and by it he being dead yet speaketh.**
>
> **Hebrews 11:4**

Even though Abel is dead, he is still speaking to us God's will and plan for man. By faith Abel gave to God the first that he had and the richest part of it. He believed that if he gave God the best that he had God would take care of him.

What Cain did was different. Cain had obviously learned that he was to bring God a sacrifice, but he didn't give God the best that he had and he certainly didn't give God the first that he had.

Tithing — An Act of Faith

This principle is still true today. God's people have been instructed to tithe. But tithing is not only a commandment of the Lord; it is an act of faith. It's the same act that placed Abel at the beginning of that "faith hall of fame."

To tithe is to bring God our firstfruits, or the first of what we have. After that comes the giving of offerings.

101

God's Attitude Toward Tithing

Not only are we to bring God a tenth, or the first of what we have, but there is something besides that. Let's look in Proverbs, chapter 3. Note the word *honour* in verse 9, and you will see God's attitude towards this. It says:

Honour the Lord with thy substance, and with the firstfruits of all thine increase:

So shall thy barns be filled with plenty, and thy presses shall burst out with new wine.

Proverbs 3:9,10

In this Scripture Solomon was instructing his son to honor the Lord. That's what Abel was doing and that's one reason why God received his sacrifice. Abel did it in faith and he did it as an honor to God.

Now people today who don't tithe are like Cain. They aren't operating in any faith and they are dishonoring the Lord. They have been dropping a dollar bill in the offering plate for years instead of honoring God with their firstfruits as God's Word has declared for them to do.

To Avoid Tithing Is To Rob God

God rejected Cain and accepted Abel, because of the attitude God has concerning this subject. In fact, in Malachi, chapter 3, we can see God's attitude toward another group of people who had failed to tithe. In verse 8 we read these words from God through His prophet:

Will a man rob God? Yet ye have robbed me. But ye say, Wherein have we robbed thee? In tithes and offerings.

That means God considered what Cain did to be robbery. Cain was taking from God that which rightly belonged to Him, so God rejected Cain's offering. That offering wasn't acceptable to God because it wasn't the first, it wasn't the best and it wasn't blood.

Cain Got Very Angry at Abel

Let's look again at what was said about this in Genesis, chapter 4:

> And in the process of time it came to pass, that Cain brought of the fruit of the ground an offering unto the Lord.
>
> And Abel, he also brought of the firstlings of his flock and of the fat thereof. And the Lord had respect unto Abel and to his offering:
>
> But unto Cain and to his offering he had not respect. And Cain was very wroth, and his countenance fell.
>
> **Genesis 4:3-5**

As this Scripture says, ...**Cain was very wroth, and his countenance fell.** Cain became upset and his face took on a frown. Now we know why: because God didn't receive or accept his offering, and he had really wanted God to accept it.

That's the way it is with some folks today. They won't do what God has said for them to do in His Word, but they still want God to bless them.

In effect, Cain was the first stingy man. Instead of trusting and honoring God, he kept holding onto his wallet. He was thinking to himself, *I had better keep back some of these crops, so I'll just give God this over here.* But God rejected it.

Abel did not have a Scripture that he could stand on. He didn't know how all this was going to work out, but he did it in faith. He gave God the first that he had and the best that he had.

God's Response to Cain

After Cain had gotten angry, note the Lord's response:

> And the Lord said unto Cain, Why art thou wroth? and why is thy countenance fallen?

> **If thou doest well, shalt thou not be accepted? and if thou doest not well, sin lieth at the door....**
>
> **Genesis 4:6,7**

After seeing what Cain had done, God was calling it sin. He said to Cain, **Sin lieth at the door**.

Now let's read verse 7 from *The Amplified Bible*:

> **If you do well, will you not be accepted? And if you do not do well, sin crouches at your door; its desire is for you, and you must master it.**

In other words, God was saying to Cain, "Since you are not willing to do the right thing, you are inviting sin to come inside you."

Now this Scripture is not referring to man's heart. It says, **Sin crouches at your door; its desire is for you, and you must master it.**

Satan succeeded in getting Adam and Eve to fail, so next he went after their children. That's the way he operates.

This means you have a responsibility to live right before God. If you don't, then not only will Satan get hold of you, but he will go after your children and your grandchildren.

Sin can be running through generations of families. Somebody has to be living right in God's eyes so that God can use that person to finally stand up and kick the devil off their premises.

Cain Could Have Changed

So as we saw in the beginning, Satan went after the firstborn son. Sin was crouching at the door. The first thing Cain had to do was to realize his error and change his way toward God.

In verse 7 God was saying to Cain: "It was Satan who came and spoke to your heart about operating this way. I could not accept your offering, because it was not blood or in faith; it was not the first or the best that you had. You were listening to the devil, and that will get you into trouble every time. Cain, you must resist the thoughts that you have now and the malice that is in your heart. Satan, the Wicked One, is speaking to you, so resist him!"

Resist Temptation!

Every believer must resist temptation when it comes. Temptation can be more than just sexual impurity. You can be tempted not to give when God says to give. You must resist temptation to disobey God whenever He is directing you to do a certain thing.

Satan will always be there to try to get you to disobey God. Satan knows that, when you obey God, blessings will come your way. He knows too that by getting you to disobey God he has you right where he wants you.

Look again at Genesis 4, verse 8:

And Cain talked with Abel his brother: and it came to pass, when they were in the field, that Cain rose up against Abel his brother, and slew him.

Unfortunately the *King James Version* makes it sound a little flat when it says, **Cain** *talked* **with Abel.** The actual Hebrew word translated *talked* means more than that. In the Hebrew it says, "Cain quarreled with him."[2]

The Problem of Envy

Cain fought with his brother. Why? Because he was envious. Cain was the first envious person. He envied his brother's blessing and relationship with God.

That still hasn't changed to this day. Some people are angry because they see other people being used and blessed by God more than themselves. But it can happen if they haven't been willing to do what those others have done.

Maybe you know someone who has been like Abel and has received the blessings of God, while you have been like Cain; and like Cain, you are upset about it. You need to check your attitude. Remember, sin is crouching at your door. By being envious of another's blessings, you are opening the door to Satan.

In the epistle of James we can see what happens when envy shows up and isn't resisted by the believer. Envy is a spirit from the enemy, Satan, and it must be resisted.

But if ye have bitter envying and strife in your hearts, glory not, and lie not against the truth.

This wisdom descendeth not from above, but is earthly, sensual, devilish.

James 3:14,15

The Greek word for "sensual" is *psuche*, meaning "mind, soul."[3] This kind of wisdom comes from the emotions, and it is not of God.

Envy Opens the Door
to *Every* Evil Work

Look at the next verse:

For where envying and strife is, there is confusion and every evil work.

James 3:16

Now all of us have to face envy at one time or another. When somebody gets married, we are filled with envy. When somebody is promoted to a better job than ours, we get jealous. When somebody joins a church or ministry staff full time, we become envious. Something good happens to another person and we want it, too.

You cannot allow envy to hang around; you must deal with it. Envy is a spirit and an enemy of the believer. You have to speak to envy, telling it, "In the name of Jesus, I resist you, envy! Get out of here!"

By not resisting envy, you will find that every evil work will be conjured up inside you. You could wind up doing the same thing Cain did and become a murderer because of envy. Now you might not kill another person physically by taking a gun and blowing him away, but you can kill people with the words of your mouth, by talking against them.

Let's say somebody in the church choir leads the worship service, and you complain about it, saying, "That person *always* gets to lead the singing." Maybe that's because God blessed him (or her) with a good voice and you don't have that same kind of voice. You don't have to get jealous about it.

God gives certain talents to certain people. We should praise God for their talent. God blessed them to be able to do that.

Sometimes I wish I could sing songs of praise during a church service, but it doesn't work that way. I'm not a lead singer, so I don't try to be a soloist. But I'm not envious of people who can. I don't get mad just because I can't do it. God has given me other gifts.

There is also no reason to get envious about somebody else's wife or husband. If you are single, God can give you a mate that He has made especially for you; if you are married, you need to do what God says in His Word and treat your mate accordingly. Then that person will be the best one you could ever have. Your attitude is paramount to whether Satan is able to take hold on you and get his clutches around you.

Even though you are saved, sanctified and filled with the Holy Ghost, you can still get off into areas where you don't belong if you don't stop and check for envy.

Sin Brings Death

Looking again in Genesis, chapter 4, we see that Cain was filled with envy because God had rejected his sacrifice and had accepted his brother's. As far as God was concerned, it was as if Cain was stealing, because his heart wasn't right. God wanted Cain to get his heart right, to do the right thing and to obey what he was told by his parents. Cain's brother did, but Cain would not.

In verse 7 God was saying to him, "If you do the right thing, won't I accept you?"

Then in verse 8 we see that Cain quarreled with his brother:

> **And Cain talked with Abel his brother: and it came to pass, when they were in the field, that Cain rose up against Abel his brother, and slew him.**

Because of sin, the manifestation of death came right away. But as we have read in Hebrews 11:4, Abel is still testifying to people today.

Be Like Abel

God intends for believers to read about this story in Genesis and learn from it.

God expects us to be like Abel when we give our tithes and offerings to Him. We are to give the best that we have of all the fruit He has given to us. We are to give not only of our financial resources, but the best of *all* that we have: our time, our talents, our abilities.

As we do, God's blessings will be manifested in our lives.

God's Plan for Provision

We know that the first thing God gave to man was dominion and authority over all the earth. The second thing God gave man was seed.

"Seeding Seed"

In Genesis 1:29 God said to Adam:

> **Behold, I have given you every herb bearing seed....**

The center cross reference in my Bible shows that the Hebrew rendering for the phrase, *herb bearing seed*, is "seeding seed."

Here is what God was saying to Adam: "I am going to give you two things. By these two things, you will have your life sustained. Number one, I give you authority over everything in this earth; and number two, I give you seeding seed." The phrase, *seeding seed*, represents provision.

The Farmer's Best Seed

If you know anything about farming, you know that seeding seed to the farmer is seed that is kept back for planting. It's his best seed.

When a crop comes in, the first thing the farmer does is to look over his crop and pick out the best part of it. He then takes that crop and stores it in his barn. That portion is not to be consumed by him or sold to the market. It is to be kept as seed for the next year's harvest.

The worst thing a farmer can do is to go through his cornfields, look at all the crop and put aside the poorest of it, saying, "This isn't very good, so I'll just stick it in the barn and plant it again next year."

If he did that, what would happen? His crop would keep degenerating until it was absolutely useless. That would not be a provision for him.

The farm products we buy in the supermarket are never the best. The best was kept in the barn to be replanted the next year. That's the seeding seed. The farmer looks through his fields for the best and juiciest kernels of corn, and that becomes his seeding seed.

Our Seeding Seed Is the Tithe

This is the reason God wants the tenth of our income off the top. That's our seeding seed.

Don't be spending your money on what you desire, saying, "If there's any left over, I'll give it to God."

By giving God only what is left, you wouldn't be presenting Him with your seeding seed. You would be giving Him some of that old "corn" that you weren't going to use anyway. After doing that, you can't be blaming God because you aren't getting the maximum results.

The Seed Must Be Planted

Notice what God did for Adam. First, He gave him authority; then He gave him seed. That's all God gave to Adam. And notice something else: God didn't plant Adam's seed for him; He expected Adam to do it.

God was saying to him: "I am giving you authority, and I am giving you seed. The authority and the seed give you the ability to determine your own destiny based upon the seed that you sow. If you don't sow this seed, you will die."

Now it was not God's plan for Adam to die. If Adam ate that seed, he would have no provision. If he wasted the seed, he would have no provision. If all he did was to preserve the seed, he would have no provision.

When you have been given seed, there is only one way you will have provision: by planting that seed. When the harvest comes up, you are to take the best part of that harvest and set it aside. It becomes your seeding seed for the next year's provision. Then when harvesting the next year's crop, you put aside your seeding seed and replant it when ready. Every year of your life you will be getting results — God's best!

God established this principle, and that's the way He expects you to live. But remember, God is not going to plant your seed for you.

Endnotes

[1]Strong, "Hebrew," p. 39, #2459.

[2]*The Holy Bible, King James Version.* (Camden, NJ: Thomas Nelson, 1972), p. 4, footnote #8.

[3]Strong, "Greek Dictionary of the New Testament," p. 79, #5590.

11

Satan's Temptations

As we have already learned, Satan gained control of this planet after Adam and Eve had sinned against Almighty God. It was Satan who preyed on Cain and caused him to kill his brother, Abel.

The God of This World

According to Second Corinthians, chapter 4, Satan became the god of this world. It says:

> ...the god of this world hath blinded the minds of them which believe not, lest the light of the glorious gospel of Christ, who is the image of God, shall shine unto them.
>
> 2 Corinthians 4:4

Note the lowercased "g" in the phrase, **the god of this world**, as opposed to the capitalized "G" in **God**, meaning Almighty God.

We know that the Father God is not blinding people to His Gospel. It is Satan, the god of this world, who works at that job. As mentioned previously, Adam had once been "the god of this world." The only thing Adam could not do was to go against what God had told him. But Satan became the god of this world through Adam's disobedience to God's command.

Jesus Was Tempted

In chapter 4 of Luke's gospel, we see Satan's temptations of Jesus. After Jesus had been baptized in the Jordan River and was anointed by the Holy Ghost, He was led of the Spirit into the wilderness. Then He was tempted of the devil for forty days and forty nights. (vv. 1,2.)

I want you to notice what Satan said to Jesus after He had come through those forty days of temptations:

...And in those days he did eat nothing: and when they were ended, he afterward hungered.

And the devil said unto him, If thou be the Son of God, command this stone that it be made bread.

Luke 4:2,3

The first thing Satan did was to try the same trick on Jesus that he had tried on Eve. He said to Jesus, *If* **thou be the Son of God....** In other words, he was asking Jesus, "Did God *really* say this? Is this *really* the way it is?"

Jesus responded to the devil by quoting from Old Testament Scripture, found in Deuteronomy 8:3.

And Jesus answered him, saying, It is written, That man shall not live by bread alone, but by every word of God.

Luke 4:4

Satan Offered Kingdom Power to Jesus

Then Satan attacked Jesus from another angle:

And the devil, taking him up into an high mountain, shewed unto him all the kingdoms of the world in a moment of time.

And the devil said unto him, All this power [all the kingdoms of the world] will I give thee, and the glory of them: for that is delivered unto me; and to whomsoever I will I give it.

If thou therefore wilt worship me, all shall be thine.

Luke 4:5-7

Note that Jesus did not refute Satan's claim of ownership over the kingdoms of this world. It was the truth.

Being described as a temptation of Jesus, this certainly could not have been a temptation if it were something Jesus already had. If Jesus had been in control of this world, it would not have tempted Him for Satan to have come to Him and said, "I will give You this power if You will fall down and worship me."

Jesus did not contradict what Satan said; He just told Satan to get behind Him:

> **And Jesus answered and said unto him, Get thee behind me, Satan: for it is written, Thou shalt worship the Lord thy God, and him only shalt thou serve.**
> **Luke 4:8**

As the god of this world, Satan has a legal right to be here until Adam's lease runs out. Adam had been given dominion over this world until a new heaven and a new earth would come into existence. Then Satan took possession of Adam's lease.

But there is a certain class of people on the earth that Satan has no power or authority over: the Body of Christ; that is, unless they allow him that authority. Because the devil had no authority over Jesus, he couldn't stop Jesus at any time. But Jesus didn't refute the fact that Satan had the right to be here.

The Devil Quoted Scripture

Then the devil came at Jesus again. This time he tried to be really sly by quoting Scripture to Jesus:

> **And he brought him to Jerusalem, and set him on a pinnacle of the temple, and said unto him, If thou be the Son of God, cast thyself down from hence:**
>
> **For it is written, He shall give his angels charge over thee, to keep thee:**
>
> **And in their hands they shall bear thee up, lest at any time thou dash thy foot against a stone.**

And Jesus answering said unto him, It is said, Thou shalt not tempt the Lord thy God.

And when the devil had ended all the temptation, he departed from him for a season.

Luke 4:9-13

By dangling suicide in Jesus' face, Satan was trying to get Him to tempt God. Satan said to Him, "If You are God, then throw Yourself off this pinnacle. If You are Who You say You are, then God will protect You." He wanted Jesus to commit suicide. But suicide is not of God.

Satan Is the Destroyer

Satan as the god of this planet is involved in all kinds of things that Almighty God is getting the blame for.

Insurance policies describe an earthquake or a flood as "an act of God." When a flood comes and people are killed, the news media will say, "It was an act of God that wiped out thousands of homes."

But that wasn't an act of God. God is not the One Who did it. Jesus drew the line in John 10:10 when He said, **The thief cometh not, but for to steal, and to kill, and to destroy.** Satan is that thief.

Satan is the one who takes people's lives. When those people are unlearned in the Word of God, he knows God will get the blame. They will hate God and ask questions like, "Why did God destroy the house I worked so hard to build?" or "Why did God take away my job?"

But God didn't do any of those things; Satan is the one responsible. Satan doesn't want people having anything to do with God. He is the destroyer, the tempter, the one Jesus came to annihilate. And that's what Jesus did on the cross: He annihilated the devil and took back the keys of death and hell. (Rev. 1:18.)

12
Choose God!

You need to realize that God has a plan and a purpose for your life. He has a design for you. He has an anointing for you. He has a work for you to do. He has a ministry for you to fill. But the choices you make will determine whether you get to do what God intends for you to do.

What choice are you going to make in this present life?

As the prophet Elijah said to God's people:

> **How long halt ye between two opinions? if the Lord be God, follow him: but if Baal, then follow him. And the people answered him not a word.**
>
> **1 Kings 18:21**

In other words, Elijah was saying to them: "Why do you hold between two opinions? You can't have it both ways. If God be God, then serve Him; but if Baal be your god, then serve him."

Baal was a type of the world, a type of sin, a type of man doing things the humanistic way to gratify his own flesh.

So you have to make up your mind:

Which God are you going to serve?

Whose plan are you going to follow?

Are you going to do things God's way or your own humanistic way?

Are you going to find out what God's Word says about things in this life and then choose His plan, or are you going to allow other factors to determine your choice?

117

If you want to live holy before God, then you have to get out of sin. You have to do what God tells you and stop stumbling around! If God has called you to the ministry, then go to work. If God has given you a work to do, then get at it.

Believer's Authority Over Satan

Have you received Jesus as your Lord and Savior? If not, you can do it now. Receiving Jesus is easy to do.

You need to recognize that you are a sinner and are being dominated by the god of this world, Satan. By accepting the blood of Jesus as the sacrifice for your sins, you can become born again. Then God will take you from spiritual death to spiritual life.

Your life can be changed right now by praying this simple prayer from your heart:

"Jesus, I know I'm a sinner. I know I'm lost, but I want You to come into my heart and save me. So I receive you now as my Savior and I make You the Lord of my life."

Now you have been born again supernaturally!

As Scripture says:

Therefore if any man be in Christ, he is a new creature: old things are passed away; behold, all things are become new.

2 Corinthians 5:17

The last phrase of this verse in *The Amplified Bible* says, **Behold, the fresh and new has come!**

Another translation says, "He is a new species of being that never before existed."

Now you have the power of the name of Jesus and the sword of the Spirit, which is the Word of God, and you can be filled to overflowing with the Holy Ghost. God's Word says, **He** [the Holy Spirit] **Who lives in you is greater (mightier) than he** [the devil] **who is in the world** (1 John 4:4 AMP).

Guess what? The god of this world no longer has any dominion over you. Because you are now born of God, you are able to resist the devil. God's Word says, **Submit yourselves therefore to God. Resist the devil, and he will flee from you** (James 4:7).

God's intention is that mankind be out from under Satan's boot. By reversing roles, you can now put your boot on his neck and keep him underfoot!

About the Author

Keith Butler is the founder and pastor of Word of Faith International Christian Center in Detroit, Michigan, which was begun on January 14, 1979, and now has a congregation of well over 13,000 members. He also pastors Faith Christian Center in College Park, Georgia, which began in August, 1993 and Faith Christian Center in Phoenix, Arizona which was founded in September, 1997.

Bishop Butler is a pastor and Bible teacher who ministers in seminars, conventions and churches throughout the country. His ministerial emphasis is on teaching line by line, with instruction on how God's Word can be applied to daily living. His television and radio ministry, "The Living Word," reaches into several states.

Bishop Butler and his lovely wife, Deborah, have three children who assist them in ministry: Pastor Keith A. Butler, II, Ms. Michelle Butler, and Ms. Kristina Butler.

To contact Bishop Butler,
write:

Bishop Keith A. Butler
P. O. Box 760037
Lathrup Village, Michigan 48076-0037
1-888-909-WORD

*Please include your prayer requests and comments
when you write.*

Additional copies of this book
and another book by Keith Butler,
Success Strategies From Heaven,
are available from your local bookstore.

HARRISON HOUSE
Tulsa, Oklahoma 74153

In Canada, books are available from:

Word Alive
P. O. Box 670
Niverville, Manitoba
CANADA R0A 1E0

The Harrison House Vision

Proclaiming the truth and the power
Of the Gospel of Jesus Christ
With excellence;

Challenging Christians to
Live victoriously,
Grow spiritually,
Know God intimately.